The Landscape of Waste

Alberto Bertagna
Sara Marini

The Landscape of Waste

with contributions by
Renato Bocchi
Giovanni Corbellini
Enrico Fontanari

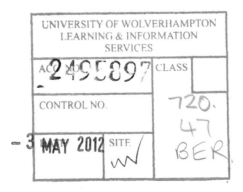

Cover
Michele Lamanna, from the
series *Paesaggio negato*,
2009–11
© Michele Lamanna

Back Cover
Michele Lamanna, *Agosto
2010*
© Michele Lamanna

Design
Marcello Francone

Editorial Coordination
Vincenza Russo

Editing
Doriana Comerlati

Layout
Paola Ranzini

Translations
Just!Venice

First published in Italy in 2011 by
Skira Editore S.p.A.
Palazzo Casati Stampa
via Torino 61
20123 Milano
Italy
www.skira.net

© 2011 The authors for their texts
© 2011 Università Iuav di Venezia
© 2011 Skira editore

Printed and bound in Italy. First edition

ISBN: 978-88-572-0852-7

Distributed in USA, Canada, Central & South
America by Rizzoli International Publications,
Inc., 300 Park Avenue South, New York,
NY 10010, USA.
Distributed elsewhere in the world by Thames
and Hudson Ltd., 181A High Holborn,
London WC1V 7QX, United Kingdom.

This book has been supported by the Italian
Ministry of Education, University and
Research, through the programme PRIN 2007
(Research Project of National Interest;
Research Unit University Iuav of Venice;
*Waste Archipelagos. Investigation on the
Relationship between Waste and Design*)
and by the University Iuav of Venice through
the Research Unit *Refused and Abandoned
Landscapes. Design Strategies of Recycling.*

Contents

10   Too Quiet a Solitude.
Building from Waste
Sara Marini and Alberto Bertagna

22   Placements.
Architectures of a Neo-Neorealism
Sara Marini

50   The Waste Land-scape.
Fragments of Thought for a Hypothesis
of Landscape as Palimpsest
Renato Bocchi

64   Residuals
Giovanni Corbellini

82   Urban Arrangements
Enrico Fontanari

102   Digestions.
Separate Project Collection
Alberto Bertagna

126   Biographies

127   Captions

"Rare books perish in my press, under my hands,
yet I am unable to stop their flow:
I am nothing but a refined butcher."

Bohumil Hrabal

Sara Marini and Alberto Bertagna

Too Quiet a
Building fro

olitude.
n Waste

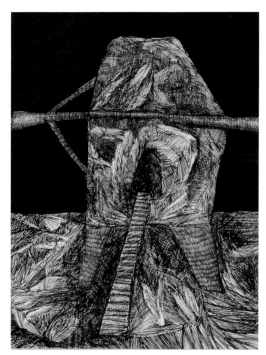

Though the mechanical press with which Hanta compacts books, like waste paper, to make sealed bales is originally a tool of final elimination and oblivion, he uses it secretly to regenerate, at least temporarily, the meaning and value of the landscapes found in the unsuspecting volumes. Hence, the press becomes the vehicle of a new testimony: "Such wisdom as I have has come to me unwittingly, and I look on my brain as a mass of hydraulically compacted thoughts, a bale of ideas."[1] At first a professional of his own final demise, Hanta becomes the master of a new course for waste, as well as its consumer. The solitude he experiences in the warehouse where he has been working "for thirty-five years" is filled with the loud noise of an unceasingly renovated narration. No collective catharsis, no redemption from waste, no celebration of recycling; perhaps only the revelation of the silence necessarily imposed by waste, as renunciation, or the discontinuation of a discourse. Hanta, on the other hand, continues to tirelessly select—from that undifferentiated mass of waste paper, books and prints—those elements upon which his gaze arbitrarily lingers, the elements that attract his attention without any apparent reason, giving them freedom and placing them wide-open at the core of each new bale.

At this point, *placements*, *repetitions*, *multiplications*, *arrangements*, *decompositions* (keywords of the five essays in this book) become possible paths traced by a story of waste imagined as being endless and always about to redefine itself thanks to progressive shifts, interrupted detours or crossroads, apparent reverses or sudden advances. Signs which insist on a given trace to reconfigure it, re-signify it, or even distort or deny it.

The awareness of position relativity—that is, the relativity of each *placement*—results in the possibility of reconfiguring substance not by modifying it, but by simply dis-locating it, moving it, or by moving oneself in space and time. Transforming the acceptation of the word "landscape" so as to make it increasingly inclusive of entities, which were previously neglected or relegated to the space of an opposition to what used to qualify landscape itself, and to the time of a negativity that needs to be overcome; progressively turning one's attention towards waste rather than work; designing a city by defining open spaces rather than volumes—planes of observation or simply surfaces that leave room for manoeuvre: all these are essentially operations of collocation. Given an established practice or an imposed coordinate, the action that anticipates the project—the projection of a found element into a different scenario—consists of a change in point of view, perhaps in order to focalize the rear rather than the main facade, to take a better, deeper, closer, or more comprehensive look, to observe nature's large constructions/large-scale environmental constructions and, from there, set the frames for new systems and arrangements. The landscape originates from the desire to climb Mount Ventoux in order to look at the land from a distance. The peasant who accompanies Petrarch there does not understand this because, by contrast, his work on the land takes place at close range: he is used to a close-up approach. The terms "waste" and "landscape" share a subjective interpretation; the *ex ante* determination of the parameters involved, which are often signified by their reciprocal difference. On the Ventoux, the construction of a landscape consists of giving preference to a scene; the decision to opt for a specific position is initially an exploratory attempt which then becomes selective. Instead, if our gaze is set to a distance to the power of 10, as in Charles and Ray Eames' video *Powers of Ten*, we can travel through the infinite and the infinitesimal at the same time, thus finding the meeting points between micro- and macroscopic and choosing to avoid the fixity of a scene in favour of the perception of its unfolding.

Choice gives rise to a second possible flexion of starting from waste to go back and reflect on the project. The concept of waste implies making a selection or choice; that is, separating the useful from the useless, and the worthy from the worthless—or the no longer worthy. Separate collection represents a further step: it is a selection of what we have decided is useless, the distinction of singularity from the formless mass of the indistinct. Without assigning any value, Hanta carries out the *decomposition* of a complex, releasing singular distinct directions for each component: "Besides, I'm the only one on earth who knows that deep in the heart of each bale there's a wide-open *Faust* or *Don Carlos*, that there, buried beneath a mound of blood-soaked cardboard, lies a *Hiperion*, there, cushioned on piles of cement bags rests a *Thus Spake Zarathustra*; I'm the only one on earth who knows which bale has Goethe, which Schiller, which Hölderlin, which Nietzsche."

Amidst placements and decompositions other landscapes are designed. Based on homogeneity or difference, complexes of similar waste are rebuilt in a search for types and the nature of the material found. Consequently, staggering lists and endless multiplications are drawn up from elements that have something in common but are never identical, or room is made for repetition. We dispose and, by disposing, we highlight.

The parking lots photographed by Edward Ruscha, the industrial archaeological sites portrayed by Bernd and Hilla Becher, the waste purchased and displayed by Gordon Matta-Clark, and the houses—all almost identical—in Dan Graham's *Homes for America* are not only collections of waste, but also collector's works and, as such, exceptional in the unlimited number of items available. The "almost identical" reveals both the specificity of the places and, at the same time, the universality of the phenomena. By hoarding homogeneous signals, we discover a reality, its nature, as well as the need to reinterpret its sliding into disuse. In architecture, the similarity of repeated elements means recognition: the type and the archetype; in non-architecture, such as in Graham's *America*, waves of identical houses highlight the standardization of desires, as well as the wish to differ, but only a

VENEZIA

IL PONTE DI *RIALTO*

PONTE DI RIALTO

INGREDIENTI

PIETRA D'ISTRIA,
LEGNO, PIOMBO.

CONSUMARE PREFERIBILMENTE
PRIMA IL TEMPO DELLA ROVINA

DOPO L'APERTURA CONSERVARE
L'AMBIENTE NELLA PROPRIA ME.
SI CONSIGLIA DI FARE
DELLE FOTOGRAFIE

PRODOTTO DA VENEZIA (VE)
ITALIA

VENEZIA

414,573211 km² e

Bene protetto
dall'UNESCO

VENE

IL PONTE DI

little, from a shared feeling. Even a forgotten story or a book due to be pulped can lead to a new tale through its *repetition*. Like exercises in style or attempt-projects in which the line proceeds to insistently seek the most appropriate site, repetition can lead to the transformation of the narration itself: a slow transformation induced by a change in context or in the interlocutor. Redesigning the projects for Venice that never got beyond the planning stage will necessarily remind us of them while, at the same time, betraying them, translating them by redrawing them with a different handwriting. Drawing on textual passages means constructing a dissimilar path and finding new meanings.

*M*ultiplications, on the other hand, are the result of chasing the term "waste," of establishing acceptations which, read in dictionaries or bibliographical summaries, reveal different tools, distinct works and fates, and ambivalent meanings. In this case, observers make definitions based on difference and not homogeneity, tracing dividing lines even when there is a single entry word; they will follow the origins, the stories and their development, and will draw cobwebs of meaning, starting from a single point, through the logic of construction—the subtle balance of a line strung to connect two distinct positions. In the work of entomologists, the classification of species is instrumental to knowing an era, and thus controlling the elements present and their possible disappearance; likewise, the multiplication of scenarios and usages of a word relates a story of balances and unbalances, the arrangement and mutation of a system.

Finally, as revealed by its possible *arrangements*, the same complex of elements—elements that no longer underlie the progress of a word's meaning, but are considered in unison, at the same time and in the same space, here and now—lends itself to the definition not of lists, but rather full-fledged narrations, although unstable, freed as they are from the rigidity of a single given direction. As permanent works—depending on their setup, museological project or context—

the same elements can take on new roles, give testimony, or develop different stories according to their spatial arrangement. Material from the past, which has suffered the action of time and today presents itself as memory, can—through new arrangements—return to being the living substance of a project. In this case too the action does not manifest itself by modifying matter, but rather, as in *placements*, by altering it without distortion, affecting the object even only temporarily, highlighting hidden possibilities and revealing them through a logical concatenation which later, in a different arrangement, may accentuate others. It is a game in which the number of pawns does not vary but assume different meanings depending on the way they are arranged, according to different designs, thus proposing different stories.

Each of these five stories evokes with its specific path the possible traces of waste, interrupting too quiet a solitude. They put waste back on the scene, possibly isolated in its multiple variations and not necessarily contained in one single discourse but, instead, deprived of the univocal character of determination, and consequently, perhaps even for the same reason, free of the need to assume specified roles. Left in its substance, waste is therefore readmitted to the use of the word and newly covered as landscape. "Last month they delivered nearly fifteen hundred pounds of 'Old Masters' reproductions, dropped nearly fifteen hundred pounds of sopping-wet Rembrandts, Halses, Monets, Manets, Klimts, Cézannes, and other big guns of European art into my cellar, so now I frame each of my bales with reproductions, and when evening comes and the bales stand one next to the other waiting in all their splendour for the service elevator, I can't take my eyes off them: now *The Night Watch*, now *Saskia*, here *Le Déjeuner sur l'herbe*, there the *House of the Hanged Man at Anvers* or *Guernica*."

[1] Bohumil Hrabal, *Too Loud a Solitude*, trans. Michael Henry Heim (New York: Harcourt, 1992), p. 2. Subsequent quotes are taken from pp. 5–6.

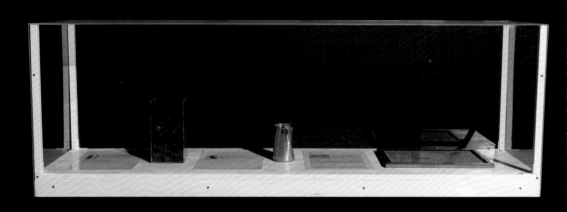

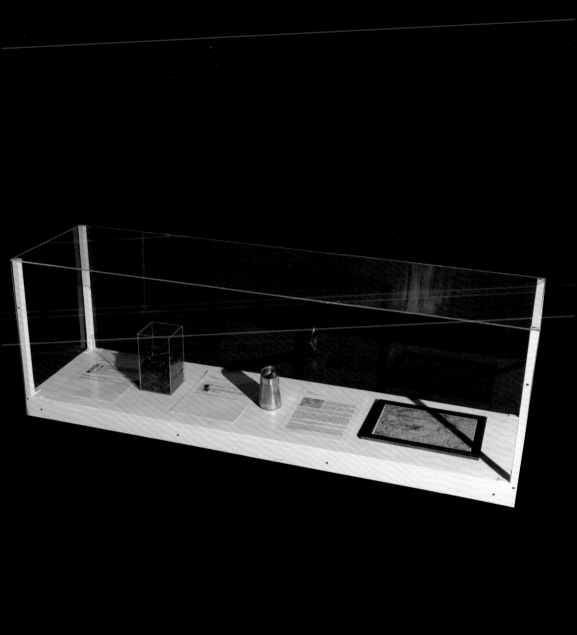

Sara Marini

Placeme

Architec

Neo-Neo

ts.

ures of a

ealism

Peter Handke "Alone in the room, he found every thing re-arranged. He turned on the faucet. A fly immediately fell off the mirror into the sink and was washed down at once. He sat down on the bed: just now that chair had been to his right, and now it was to his left. Was the picture reversed? He looked at it from left to right, then from right to left. He repeated the look from left to right; this look seemed to him like reading."[1]

Cedric Price "In the early twenty-first century big cities are finding that big users no longer require big HQs with big 'named' buildings—rather they are tending to prefer anonymous space, that can be leased and CHANGED. Unfortunately it is not a new-found modesty on the part of the big corporations but a move from the particular to the anonymous (space). For the very word SPACE is being changed by the users into COMMUNICATOR—the very need for cities is getting the thumbs down from the users themselves. Process, not Product, is the call I hear."[2]

I f you look up "placements" in the virtual network it will send you back to the position occupied in it. The association between position and virtual map seems rather paradoxical given that there is nothing less physical than the Internet and nothing less definable in terms of relative relations, but maybe this is just the result of a kind of "nostalgia for space" rather than a truth. Virtual placement is a parameter measuring visibility: unlike the strategical approaches used in the art of war, here the best position is the most visible one. The network offers a series of identical, democratic spaces: they are all screens, video dimensions, images with no precise measurements, a horizontal world where frequency defines possible rankings of success, deciding whether a position is optimum or not. *Process* and not *product* wrote Cedric Price, the author of *Fun Palace*, a building in the form of communication based on the uncertainty of its own position and of the relationship between the various parts: the important thing is the choice of movement, of what one wants to look at, of how one wants to use space. A non-systemic multidirectional architecture where the position is impossible to calculate and unstable, measurable only in statistical terms of frequency.

These two "figures," the virtual network of the Internet and the physical one of the *Fun Palace*, where the position is independent of space and its coordinates, or rather, especially in Price's work, space is placed in the background, represent vertigos, deviations of planning and production culture, in a phase of change that made the position its basic tenet, stripping bare and revealing the object, not the process, and above all, in a total reversal, hiding the rest, the product waste.

Recent newspaper headlines remind us that the element of truth, the litmus test of postmodern society is not the product but its negative: after rigorous complex analyses carried out to track down the E. Coli killer bacteria that terrorized Germany and the rest of Europe, health inspectors dug through the rubbish of one of the families struck down by the bacteria, using an age-old police procedure that allowed them to discover the truth.

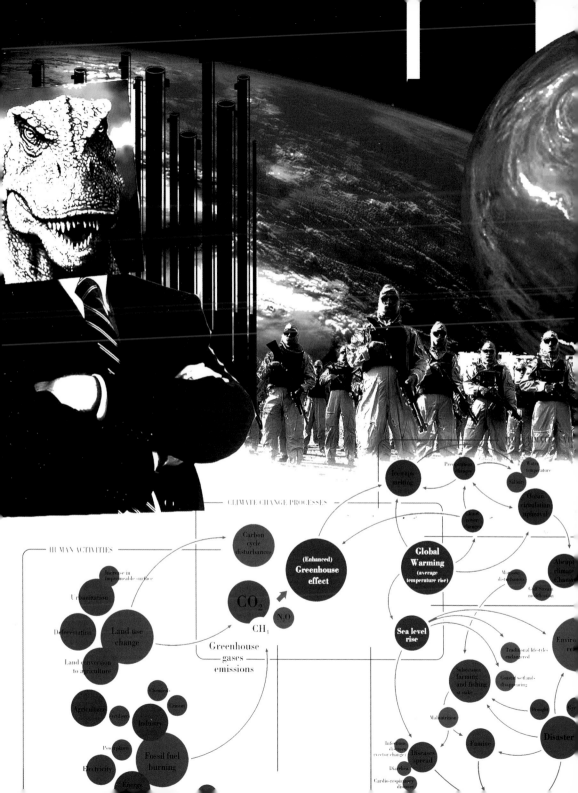

CLIMATE CHANGE PROCESSES

HUMAN ACTIVITIES

Carbon
cycle
disturbances

(Enhanced)
Greenhouse
effect

Global
Warming
(average
temperature rise)

Increase in
impermeable surface

Urbanization

CO_2

N_2O

CH_4

Deforestation

Land use
change

Greenhouse
gases
emissions

Land conversion
to agriculture

Chemicals

Cement

Agriculture

Fertilizers

Industry

Power plants

Fossil fuel
burning

Electricity

Energy

Ice caps
melting

Precipitation
change

Water
temperature

Salinity

Ocean
circulation
upheaval

Sea level
rise

Abrupt
climatic
change

Gulf Stream
modification

More
disturbances

Traditional life-style
endangered

Environ
re

Subsistence
farming and fishing
at stake

Coastal wetland
disappearing

Drought

Malnutrition

Infectious
disease
(vector change)

Famine

Disaster

Diseases
spread

Diarrhea

Cardio-respiratory
disease

Waste as a revealing force is one of the possibilities that gives rise to the value of placement: reflecting on the position implicit in the value of a term may mean finding uncertainty there. As Paul Auster points out in his *New York Trilogy* words can change their meaning or fall out of use if their meaning no longer corresponds to the thing to which they refer. Deterioration appears like a revelation, a movement, change of position, the position relative to an object that consequently requests that of the observer. Waste becomes a way of exposing the process and verifying its virtuosity. We can examine the procedure involved by breaking it down into three stages and analysing three possible positions: waste as a list in the construction of inventories; waste as an occasion for overturning the rules, like a reflecting open field; and finally waste as a new reverse-angle shot of the project, in its narration of stories despite the attention of the observer: stories that proceed without a stage.

The theme of "placement" implicit in the term "waste" raises a further question relative to scale and dimension. Usually, conventionally, waste is something that is inconspicuous, hidden, abandoned, forgotten, often fragmented, reduced to dust and therefore minuscule. The work or the product, on the other hand, flaunt themselves, advertising their presence, communicating their existence through large extensions. Today waste proposes itself as an antagonist to excess, its centrality also represents a response to what was defined as the "new dimension" in the 1960s, then rediscovered, manipulated and reviewed in the "bigness" of Rem Koolhaas. Its presence, but above all its centrality, in the contemporary debate seem to bear witness to a request for attention to the minute, to what has lost its meaning because it is part of a whole, but in its multiplication, in its being placed and interpreted in succession, it acquires dignity as a work, new meaning thanks to its serialization: differences emerge through comparison, invitations to look carefully. The state of abandonment of the Gulliver's Kingdom Theme Park built ten years ago on Mount Fuji in Japan seems to express, metaphorically and otherwise, the victory of the Lilliputians who are trying to change the scene by slowly eroding it.

CATALOGUES OF REALITY

Jean Baudrillard "It is not that there is no remainder. But this remainder never has an autonomous reality, nor its own place: it is what partition, circumscription, exclusion designate... what else? It is through the substraction of the remainder that reality is founded and gathers strength... what else?"[3]

Various studies in the field of observation and projects describe the nature of empty spaces, or *spazi di risulta*, as the result of the construction of a precise plan. As suggested by Georges Perec in *Life: A User's Manual*, their serial presence at local level allows us to interpret them using an approach similar to that adopted in biological research: classifications, lists and collections make the "rest" meaningful in its dishomogeneous repetitiveness. Perec, one of the upholders of the "rediscovery of the real" constructed his novel-essay on the image of a cross-section of a building that exposes the life taking place inside. This image alludes to the representation of the nineteenth-century city which reveals its own new structures, even subterranean ones, because the reasoning of that particular culture was based on the system and construction of its useful parts without the hierarchies imposed by perspective or a selective gaze. In Perec's work the cross-section becomes a way of stripping the ordinary bare, an exposure of the contradictions and relations between interior and juxtapositions of interiors, an instrument for observing, for reasoning about and decomposing structures, fundamentally for narrating the building as a collection of lives, an antique shop of humanity.[4]

In the 1960s Edward Ruscha published *Thirtyfour Parking Lots in Los Angeles*, a photographic investigation of the city's outdoor parking lots. His cataloguing activity produced an atlas of empty places, wide expanses within the city plan constantly awaiting occupation. Ruscha documents these presences, objectively restoring them, and this detachment, combined with the emptiness of the spaces, turns into a critical comment expressed by a simple exploration of the construction mechanisms of the urban system. No longer the negation of an affirmation, in this work waste assumes the "value" of an element that must be read in its repetitiveness: rather than adopting an explanatory approach, this sampling of parking lots is "typological." By isolating the object in the frame, the photography heightens its anonymity while proposing different fictitious variants through the seriality of the shots. Presented objectively, in an almost abstract manner, in their unoccupied condition, these spaces lacking history, with little thought and planning, appear as evidence of the ordinary: repeated intervals become words in the tale of the city.[5]

In 1966 Dan Graham produced a two-page article "Homes for America" for *Arts Magazine* examining the serial city that had begun to colonize the suburbs. This project owes its fame to the fact that it depicted places in no way considered worthy of artistic representation with a precision allowing them to undergo an actual anatomical dissection. Although long confined to photography magazines, Graham's project represents one of the first critical gazes, a criticity based on silence, on the neutral observation of a reality that is now, in its multiple declensions, the subject of town-planning.

In 1967 Gordon Matta-Clark documented "gutterspaces" left over by zoning in Queens and these real residues, real in spatial and legal terms and therefore in economic terms, are the subject of *Reality Properties: Fake Estates*. The American artist builds up his own art object out of the documentation resulting from the purchase of these slivers of land: deeds, land register maps and photos. The assemblage of these materials expresses the "non sense" of the ordering process that gave rise to "useless" strips of land resulting from division and subtraction operations that nonetheless have a market value. The work highlights two of the main planning instruments dealing with waste: regulations and projects. The intensification of planning both within the city and in its hinterland, the double exposure that they may experience, is reflected in the fragmentation of land, the generation of residual zones or of meaningless "leftovers."[6]

Bern and Hilla Becher photographed over fifty industrial archaeological sites in the Ruhr basin and Sigen area, organizing and exhibiting their images by typology: silos, gasometers, blast furnaces,

Toboggan Glacier (Alaska, USA) **1909**
lat. 61° 01' 17"   long. 148° 27' 69"

Toboggan Glacier (Alaska, USA) **2(**
lat. 61° 01' 17"   long. 148° 27' 69"

mines and water towers. Also in this case the work focused on arranging and cataloguing these abandoned sites, using the same approach adopted by scientists and biologists in their studies.

These scenes propose an unexpected position of wastes. Positioned as inappropriate works, remains of works, elevated to language by a typological cataloguing not usually adopted for them: as a list, as if their repetition, their anonymous reoccurrence across the land could be, and clearly it is, evidence of the forms of the project, their taking shape, their becoming reality. Yet again the anatomical analysis to which the city is subjected in these experiences gives rise to the possibility, often forgotten or passed over, that it is a living body in which biological data is not a corollary but the core affecting even the inert parts of this construction in their transition from spaces in use to artefacts from an increasingly recent past.

MIRROR

Hal Foster "So too a sculptural process may prepare a photographic tableau, as in *Island within an Island* (1993) where the (de)compositional strategy of installation art sets up the photograph—in this case a miming of the Lower Manhattan skyline in the background with found debris in the foreground. Folding medium onto medium, space onto space, island onto island, Orozco often wins critical pleasures from the otherwise painful ironies of dislocation and dispersal. After the events of 11 September 2001 this work of subversive mimicry has also taken on new meaning as an image of remembrance, of coming-after and living-on."[7]

The changes in the meaning of waste, shapeless material, are present in artistic reflections and experiments where merely repositioning an object can change its role in paradoxical terms or imbue it with new significations, just like in Duchamp's *Fountain*. Also susceptible to such operations are historic artefacts, urban icons, entire cities whose forms and materials are stripped of meaning, often due to the way they offer themselves up as goods on sale, souvenir-identities to be repeated and reconstructed in any place. The very city of Venice, or rather its crystallized image, was subjected to relocation in other territories in the American and Asian continents, a dislocation described by Elizabeth Diller and Ricardo Scofidio in the work titled *Chain City*. A unique Venice is transmitted by the vision of a chain of cities: the virtual vision of a journey in the belly of this city is sublimed, melding with the journey into other different Venices, confusing observers as to their geographic coordinates. In 2008 an installation at the Corderie in the Arsenale consisted of a film that was continuous not just because it was uninterrupted but also because it comprised a single narrative thread creating projections of the Venices in Las Vegas, Tokyo, Nagoya, Macao and Doha that made the original "a city fixed in time, but fluid in space" according to the statements of Diller, Scofidio and Renfro in the Biennale catalogue and made its copies new elements of comparison that almost blur their own "successive" existences.

Operations of real relocations, actual physical deportations also concern objects that have lost value in the sites where they were built: the British bridge described by Kevin Lynch in his *Wasting Away* and its new life in America are one such example. "When a London bridge, built in 1831, had outlived its usefulness in London, an American developer purchased it and shipped the 10,000 tons of stones to the desert of Lake Havasu City, Arizona. It was reconstructed as a tourist attraction on the site of a World War II landing strip. Water was diverted from the Colorado River to make it pass under it."[8] Lynch continues by underlining the artificiality of the resignification of the bridge concerned, or rather, by underlining the sense of wonder sought and obtained by the operation. Although in both the present and past the strategy of re-location of useless objects, whose uselessness becomes a clearly stolen identity, is/was functional to the communicative role of architecture and of its articulation in the confused mesh of globalization, there is no lack of compositional reflections where it is adopted to give rise to architectural works, like for example Piero Portaluppi's *Wagristoratore* (1930) which involved transporting two train carriages to a high altitude and reassembled to form a new architecture (as the name of the work suggests).

Some authors pursue the theory that waste is a "mirror" of reality: not only is the meaning of the structure lost but it becomes unstable at the very moment when the process of re-acquisition of significance of the "rest" persists as immanence: this confuses the relationship between the parts.

"Thus the remainder refers to much more than a clear division in two localized terms, to a turning and reversible structure, an always imminent structure of reversion, in which *one never knows which is the remainder of the other*. In no other structure can one create this reversion, or this *mise-en-abyme*: the masculine is not the feminine of the feminine, the normal is not the crazy of the crazy, the right is not the left of the left, etc. Perhaps only in the mirror can the question be posed: which, the real or the image, is the reflection of the other? In this sense one can speak of the remainder as a mirror, or of the mirror of the remainder."[9]

Rachel Whiteread's *House* proposes a further reflection on waste and the way it presents itself as a connotation of identity or of the recollection of a rejected identity. *House* takes on the history of the local area and the way its inhabitants perceive it—it is the reflection of the object-residence that lingers on as a memory, asking us to reconsider the pressing colonization resulting from demolitions and new constructions taking place in London's East End today. The artist's concrete cast of the empty spaces of an abandoned terrace house translates the domestic vacuum into volume. The cast gives rise to a comparison with what was and what no longer exists. Although the local council initially accepted this enigmatic presence, it later decided to demolish the work because local residents were "disturbed" by it. The mummification of the ghost of the house converts the home from the nest of domestic privacy to eery naked monument. The work translates "absence" into a static mass, thus producing a short circuit between the real void of a recent past and the void in terms of meaning of the present.

2009

Tiny settlements scattered in various American, European and Asian capitals are described by Lynch as icons of an instability that can turn into a project: their location in abandoned sites gives rise to a treasure or artwork hunt, inviting and urging all possible spectators to investigate and travel around unknown places. "Charles Simonds made tiny clay villages for 'little people,' on the ledges and crannies of the Lower East Side of New York. From 1971 to 1976, he built 250 such places, in unexpected and vulnerable locations. Some were destroyed within the hour, most in a few days; some few lasted as long as five years. Built of tiny bricks, the houses appeared and disappeared."[10] As soon as they are completed these micro-works prepare to tackle an unknown fate where even the tiniest everyday gesture could become a reason for transience; they are designed to measure the level of attention paid to places.

At the 54th Venice Art Biennale the British pavilion is emblazoned with the words *I, Impostor*; inside is Mike Nelson's installation. It transports visitors into a corner of an abandoned city where they can walk through the interior of a house or enter the courtyard to see part of the exterior; there are traces of lives spent there but there are no inhabitants, there is a lot of dust and the air is heavy. Who is the imposter in the title? The artist who reconstructs and exhibits a reality that becomes a work thus losing its own connotations of veracity? Or the work itself which is actually empty and which, with every day that passes, appropriates the uselessness of the structures built in its interior, turning it into its own distinctive feature? Or the impostor is the visitor who crosses the city's abandoned spaces without seeing them while they experience their own, convinced that they will never ever be empty?

INSIDE

Haruki Murakami "Here is where the old Dolphin Hotel used to stand. It was the pits of a hotel. Untold others stayed there, stepped in the grooves in the floor, saw the spots on the wall. The old Dolphin Hotel had disappeared. Yet its presence lingered on. Beneath this new intercontinental Dolphin, behind it, within it. I could close my eyes and go in."[11]

The Dolphin Hotel is a hotel like many others, a "neutral" building that does not express its belonging to a place or area, but could probably be found in any big city. The protagonist of Haruki Murakami's novel *Dance Dance Dance* is a freelance journalist who is looking for Dolphin Hotel in Sapporo but finds the Hotel Dauphin in its place. The two hotels are two different buildings that seem to have just three things in common: they have replaced each other on the same ground, they are both hotels and they share the same name. The journalist is surprised by this homonymy.

The protagonist, who is also the novel's narrator, calls the old hotel the Dolphin Hotel but refers to the new hotel by its new name, Hotel Dauphin. This distinction comes into being after the journalist's first encounter with the old structure when he decides that the name describing it is inappropriate: "Sad hotels existed everywhere, to be sure, but the Dolphin was in a class of its own. The Dolphin Hotel was conceptually sorry" so he decides to rename it Dolphin Hotel. He thus brings about a kind of appropriation of space by means of his own personal name which resists changes taking place in time, absence, destruction and replacement.

In the original novel, the use of Japanese for the name of the old hotel and more international English for the modern construction guides the reader between two hotels that are distant in time but "homonyms." This distinction underlines the perception of the dizzying transformations of places and culture: where the national language metaphorically gives way to English, tradition gives way to globalization, where neglect gives way to efficiency. The protagonist recalls the Dolphin Hotel as a dingy old building when he stayed there four years beforehand. The Hotel Dauphin is an "anonymous" hotel that has strangely inherited the old name. The Dolphin Hotel is a remnant from the past, a constructed site stained by its past, where the past is to be found "in the grooves in the floor...," a place where you end up by mistake. The Hotel Dauphin is the place of the present, indifferent to situations, a copy to be put forward everywhere, disorientating in its shape but providing orientation through its huge bulk, a hotel that could bear the name of any one of a number of big hotel chains.

The succession of the two buildings echoes the "regenerative" drive of Japan where the average life-span of a building is twenty-six years. The journalist's discovery of a new, bigger building on the site of the old hotel, built as part of a complex property development programme with murky outlines, a facility immune to the signs of time, because designed not to last, is a common experience in Japan, and not just there.

Although the replacement of buildings is frenetic in Japan, the sign of its continuous projection towards the new, this process does not cancel, but lives with a strong sense of time: this is revealed by the number identifying the building in its address "often assigned on the basis of chronological construction order rather than physical adjacency."[12]

In his novel Murakami does not describe two buildings next to each other or that have succeeded each other on the same site but a confusion of space and time involving these hotels spatially rather than metaphorically. Inside, inside the Hotel Dauphin, a fragment of the Dolphin Hotel survives. The journey between the two "places" takes place in the elevator—in fact the intruder lives on an "unexpected" floor; the elevator decides whether to stop at one of the Hotel Dauphin floors or at the Dolphin Hotel floor. When the journalist ends up on the "unexpected" floor, it is not clear whether this is a real place or not. Sometimes the author supplies indications confirming that it is genuine, while other details allude to a surreal or fantastical dimension. It is left up to the reader of *Dance Dance Dance* to opt for one hypothesis or the other, to choose whether the fragment of old building really does exist inside the "international hotel." Following one of the two roads does not prevent us from undergoing interferences, a short-circuit resulting from the overlapping of two realities that logically cancel each other.

In particular, the possibility that the relationship between old and new is inspired by the nesting doll principle gives rise to a series of reflections on the two identities involved. "This is what occurs: identity is like immunity, one identifies with the other. Lowering one, lowers the other. Extraneousness and being foreign become diffused and quotidian. This translates into a constant exteriorization of myself: I need to measure, control and test myself. [...] But the most insidious enemies lie within: the old viruses have always been hidden in the shade of immunity, have always been intruders, because they have always existed."[13]

THE BRIDGEHEAD WAS DECAPITATED!
Parasitic Architecture Besiege the Liberty Bridge

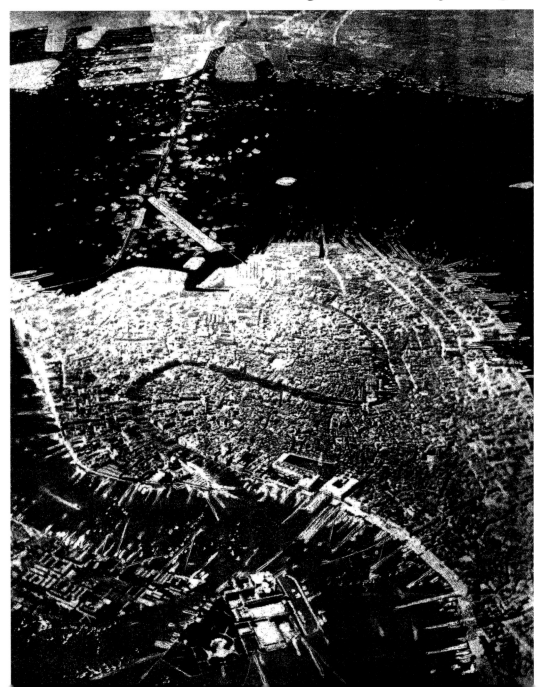

The two identities face each other by virtue of this anomalous co-existence that involves the new hotel in spite of itself. The intruder remains a confined space, distant from the present, different, meaning that crossing the "threshold" separating it from the host building signifies crossing a chronological distance. In this case darkness is the filter, darkness cancels all physical contact between the two realities, avoiding every figuration, every possible image attributable to the transition area.

The connection between the two spaces cannot be examined by means of sight therefore but implies the involvement of the rest of the body undergoing the time leap. It is the journalist's body that measures the distances, the space and time, and it is yet again his body that participates as the minimum unit of this connection without which the link would not exist. However his body is altered, only involved in the perception of the old presence. While the spaces of the present, no matter how pacific, frighten us by underlining distances and cancelling all connections.

While the public spaces of the contemporary world express their democratic nature by eliminating connotative codes, the body reacts by seeking personal references, seeking to invert roles, to stop enduring space but order it in search of a personalization, even by breaking the rules of time if necessary. Though modern architecture may have pondered on how to free the body from the dictates of space, finding a solution in the "almost nothing," that is, by reducing construction elements to the minimum and abstracting them, in the contemporary world this extreme legacy leads to an inversion of roles whereby the body seeks links and aims to lay down the rules.

The survival of a fragment of the Dolphin Hotel symbolizes an act of resistance against the neutral repeatable language of the present. In the Hotel Dauphin the protagonist allows space to numb him, a sensation frequently investigated by Japanese culture's reflections on the existential condition, which is perceived and narrated even by those outside it, like director Sophia Coppola who created her film *Lost in Translation* around this sense of alienation.

Murakami reacts to this widespread apathy with the survival of the Dolphin Hotel, the survival of a personal space, something imprinted in the memory that he calls by name and that can be given a name, that can be dragged into the present so as not to lose the connections, to respond to the indifference of the spaces of the present. The contrast between the two realities grows gradually during the protagonist's incursions into a Dolphin Hotel that becomes increasingly defined, increasingly recognizable.

The meaning of this parallel space-time is unravelled by the words of the Sheep Man, the mysterious inhabitant of the *last room* in the old hotel: "Wethoughtofeverything. Everything, so youcouldreconnect."[14]

The co-existence of the two hotels is therefore functional to a connection. Although the encounter between two realities that are logically incompatible heightens their differences, by making a greater effort, once the feeling of alienation has been left behind, the links, the cross-references remain. Leaving the obvious distances aside, the Dolphin Hotel and Hotel Dauphin are linked by the unfolding of the story, by the events, that would not have taken place had the new construction changed its name and failed to "absorb" the old one. Distances live on to the degree that the old hotel remains unchanged, true to the protagonist's memory, undergoing no restylings and facing the present.

The *anomalous* stratification of spaces described in *Dance Dance Dance* does not cancel the identities involved but heightens them by leaving them unchanged, indifferent to the presence of the other, but functional to the pursuit of a plot, a connection. Other works have explored this "confusion of space and time," using "impossible co-existences" as elements of friction that are useful for the search for forgotten links that only the body, in the presence of a given space, can manage to recall and re-process. In Ingmar Berman's *Wild Strawberries* the old doctor who is the film's protagonist finds himself physically catapulted into his memories, in this case the wild strawberry patch, where he will link past and present: although this is clearly a mental journey, the physical intrusion of the elderly protagonist into his youth in the same frame creates a feeling of alienation and an encounter that does not allow what is and what has been to be changed, but becomes more a moment of catharsis, or perhaps only of revelation. While Bergman bitterly underlines how time is running out for the protagonist of his road-movie, Murakami uses time, bending it to intertwine spaces, to re-connect, to insinuate the words of the Sheep Man: "Aslongasthemusicplays. Yougottadance!"[15]

NO STAGE

The issues of land consumption, the proliferation of buildings either abandoned or never used, a territory that appears as the waste of a ceaseless production process has led, in several European countries, to the formulation of laws limiting new construction and encouraging transformation of the existing built environment and to a search for strategies aimed at recycling space in the twentieth-century architectural debate. We are witnessing the re-proposal of a planning practice—in truth, an ancient one—defined as parasitical which entails the inclusion of new architectural bodies within pre-existing urban structures and buildings. Looking back at the last few years, we can track down a number of projects, exhibitions, structures, and initiatives evoking the term or image of a "parasite." A short chronological list of the major experiences that identify themselves with, or refer to, the parasite, clearly reveals that this strategy is not in the least exceptional. The term "parasite" indicates the ability to become *nomos*—yet always in connection with an existing element: parasitical with respect to something—and cross different disciplinary fields. Michel Serres does not define it as a simple word, but rather as a "semantic area," a "fluid" complex. The quality of being fluid and the ability to traverse environments crosswise place the "parasite" at the heart of contemporary debate, of the considerations that attempt to fix the changes that have occurred—after the crisis of the modern—in society and thought and, consequently, in the concept of space. The fluidity of the term is one of the features that has determined its success and popularity, making it an object of interest for design thinking today. This is also confirmed by the different ways in which

the word is written, stressing the *para-* suffix or not, thus implying one of the different nuances it offers. At times, it is associated with the spatial component, which remains occasional and non-position-defining in the name of that indetermination, gap, or *distance* that characterize this figure by definition.

It is in the nature of the parasite to draw life from its relationship with its host, thus leading to the negative acceptation of someone who is not self-sufficient. However, this kind of relationship does not imply the complete demise of the pre-existing, but rather a relational strategy capable of giving meaning to both parties: "lending" a meaning to the parasite and re-signifying the hosting body. A parasite provides an opportunity for resuscitating architectural "corpses," doing so driven by the pure cynicism that also characterizes it etymologically. In fact, disused places are those where it finds the greatest possibilities—in terms of both spatial and "cultural" availability—of introducing its logic and establishing change.

"In other words, each sharp observation of the real is parasitical, including the sense that it breaks the safe linearity of each assertion of truth (if anything, by attesting the temporary and contingent degree of an observation's truth). It comes before observation (and execution), without founding it; instead, it discovers the paradoxical (thus unfounded) traits every time. Each concrete action is parasitical when it fluidifies and discontinues a system's functionality: it is the occurrence of a confirmation or discontinuation."[16]

A parasite, therefore, does not found but discovers. It observes and highlights the paradoxical traits of contingency. A parasite is concrete, yet able to discontinue a system's functionality. Its aptitude for "fluidifying" given conditions, unsettling them and giving rise to indetermination, is the counterpoint to the difficulties architecture encounters when it confronts the uncertainty that characterizes contemporary times, and the spatial transformation caused by new communication media.

Since the 1980s the term "parasite" has been used in a series of studies concerning culture, design and art. For instance, Serres' *Le Parasite*, published in 1980, inspired Diller and Scofidio's work of the same name, which was displayed at the New York's Museum of Modern Art in 1989. Elizabeth Diller and Ricardo Scofidio intertwined their research with John Hejduk's thought and the work of Vito Acconci, rebuilding theories and experiences around the architectural body and organism. The *PARA-SITE* installation was constructed as a reflection on the relationship between a work and a museum and, again, between the space of the visitor and of the installation. The term "parasite" is also linked to four interrelated Dutch initiatives: the *Parasites. The City of Small Things* exhibition, the building of *Las Palmas Parasite*, the *Parasite Paradise* exhibition, and the *SchoolParasites* initiative. In 2001, in Rotterdam's year as European capital of culture, Dutch designers Korteknie and Stuhlmacher built the *Las Palmas Parasite* prototype.[17] The *Parasites. The City of Small Things* exhibition was set up inside this construction.[18] The exhibition—conceived for a show that was to take place in Sweden in 1999, also organized by the two Dutch designers—displayed proposals from the various participating architects. The works on display represented possible variations on the *p.a.r.a.s.i.t.e.* theme; that is, liveable, movable, and light structures designed for the colonization of residual urban places. The word, in this case, was an acronym: *Prototypes for Advanced Ready-made Amphibious Small-scale Individual Temporary Ecological houses and boats*.

In 2003, Leidsche Rijn, a residential neighbourhood near Utrecht, was the venue for the *Parasite Paradise* exhibition. This exhibition was part of a series of exercises in the fields of art, architecture, and urban planning taking place locally. In this case, too, the central theme was housing designed to be temporary and mobile. The term "parasite" was adopted and accompanied by the subheading: *Manifesto for Temporary Architecture and Flexible Urbanism*. The event saw the participation of international architects and artists, including Vito Acconci who submitted a work entitled *Mobile Linear City*, which opened a cycle of projects developed by his studio dedicated to the "parasite-virus" theme. The exhibition was documented in the book *Parasite Paradise* [19] which, in a retrospective concerning mobile architecture, presented Michael Rakowitz's work *paraSITE*: a transportable dwelling for the homeless and a reflection on the contemporary right to a home. Korteknie and Stuhlmacher were also invited to participate in this event with the work *Nomads in Residence*, made in collaboration with the Bik van der Pol artists. *Parasite Paradise* is a project by Beyond,[20] an organization resulting from an initiative promoted by the Utrecht Municipality, the Dutch Department of Cultural Affairs (DMO), and the Leidsche Rijn project in Utrecht of the Vinex Property Development, with the participation of the Foundation for Art and Public Space (SKOR). The two events—*Las Palmas Parasite* and *Parasite Paradise*—shared the patronage of SKOR, a national organization based in Amsterdam. Further, SKOR was also responsible, together with Korteknie and Stuhlmacher, for the *SchoolParasites* initiative.[21] Yet another opportunity for experimenting with the "parasite" theme, the event involved the construction in 2004, in Hoogvliet near Rotterdam, of three structures forming a school. The temporary need for space in school facilities in Holland is usually resolved by using containers; therefore, this initiative represented a response to how this additional space is built. Korteknie and Stuhlmacher, the curators of this project, invited three architects to create different structures meeting the needs of the users: the school children.

Finally, the term "parasite" occurs in the name of exhibition facilities—such as the *P.A.R.A.S.I.T.E. Museum of Contemporary Art* of Ljubljana and the *Para/Site Art Space* in Hong Kong—and represents the type of relationship these organizations and their facilities have established with the city.

The words in the *p.a.r.a.s.i.t.e.* acronym become possible criteria and guidelines investigating the architectural attitude founded on the co-existence of several identities. In particular, "ready-made," "individual," and "ecological" relate the principles underlying this design practice. The experiments adopting the term "parasite" express the desire to recycle space (ready-made) using it in ways that respond to actual needs (individual), and are in favour of an ecological approach towards the territory not limited to the use of alternative energy sources or the selection of building materials, but also affects the process upstream, that is, the same approach that allows us to consider built environments as being reusable and redesignable (ecological).

On the other hand, as far as the function of the object is concerned, it seems that the parasitical strategy usually responds to housing issues (houses) by presenting itself as a concrete,

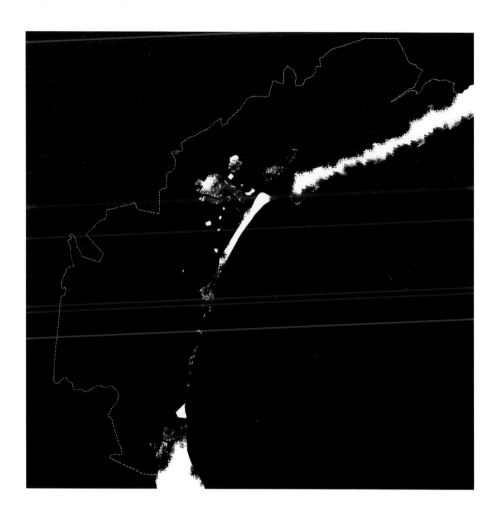

and often economically sustainable, response. However, even if this field of application is the privileged one, it is not the only one possible. The need for public space is one of the factors that cause us to embrace this way of implementing the existing, given its flexibility and ability to unsettle the clarity of existing limits. Although the experiments carried out in the field of art use this approach to the creation of public space—often, paradoxically, in an unauthorized way—in order to break the boundaries of the museum-container and to become a way of commenting on the role of art itself with respect to current city-making. Significantly the term was evoked by Korteknie and Stuhlmacher to describe how their *Parasite. The City of Small Things* was inserted into an exhibit to which the two designers were only invited once all the space had already been assigned. At that point, the two authors decided to insert their tale in the empty spaces of the exhibition, creating an itinerary parallel to that of the show.

Finally, the term "small-scale" does not simply represent a dimensional issue, but rather, as written in the introduction to the exhibition *Parasites. The City of Small Things*, an attitude towards the city and, in general, a cultural stand whereby "building" and "transformation" start from small things.

Serres clarifies the bond between the parasite, intended as interference, and the space of transformation: "Individual spots, categories or phenomena, praxes or wrought objects, placed together under the name of Hermes— these were the spaces of transformation encountered at first. Interference is an aural and visual phenomenon, a phenomenon of physics; it is a metaphor and an art of invention."[22]

Metaphor and the art of invention intersect in this image: the experiences adopting it as the manifesto of their project-development capacity veer between these two approaches. The recourse to words with a great heuristic capacity is found throughout architectural literature: let us consider, for instance, the architecture/body of work of Leonardo or of Francesco di Giorgio Martini or, in modern times, Le Corbusier's reference to the experiments carried out in the fields of aeronautical or automotive engineering, or again the image of the *bricoleur* evoked by Colin Rowe in *Collage City*, used in response to the idea of "society as a vegetable continuum" and the biological metaphor of classical origin. The term "parasite" is not simply used as a metaphor; it is also, and above all, evoked to represent an art of contingency characterizing the states of necessity, a way to meet today's needs, bringing into being, at once and without mediation, the conflicts and contradictions that flow through the city, giving them a physical character.

The following text, in the form of *notes for the decomposition of a city of labour*, is the account of a place whose location and history are marginal to this argument. What we wish to underline is the position, this time one assumed by the observer, of a searcher for new life. As Kevin Lynch repeatedly emphasizes in his *Wasting Away*, reiterated by the title of Michael Braungart's famed *Cradle to Cradle. Remaking the Way We Make Things*, the story of the abandonment of a space may correspond to an account of a continuously advancing transformation that we are powerless to halt.

GHOSTS, OR OF THE NEW GOLD. People still inhabit this place. Or rather, they thoroughly loot and pillage it; stripped cables, dismantled equipment and targeted excavations are all proof of a lively nocturnal activity that is anything but random or unstructured. A new (dis)assembly line is at work in the city in search of the new gold of the twenty-first century.

NEW BUILDINGS. As architecture's gears and components gradually decompose at the hands of time (and not just of time), new forms of life design new constructions: vegetation can finally grow undisturbed, workaholic spiders take advantage of the space available to weave their webs. The decommissioning of the site coincides with occupation by other motives: the production cycle is continuous.

TECHNOLOGY, OR ARCHAEOLOGY. Abandoned machines along with the signs and fences that instructed their usage are proof of technology's efforts to chase time and the best production methods. These self-same machines—captured in all their uselessness and evident dereliction—bring to mind the words of Vladimir Nabokov in *The Eye*: "It is amusing to catch another's room by surprise. The furniture froze in amazement when I switched on the light."[23] A "jesting fate" seems to assign them the role of witnesses, not so much to progress, but to ancient worlds. As Bruno Munari points out in *Fossili del 2000*: witnesses to be placed in a showcase, archaeological finds from a recent past despite themselves.

SKIES. Usually the value of a building is associated with its façades, which represent its frame of communication towards the city. In other cases, it is based on the arrangement of its spaces, the different heights, the design of its section, on the belly of its architecture. In this place the value lies in the skies, as the roofing helplessly witnesses the transformation below, in spite of the abandonment. As the rest of the structure decays, the flows dictated by the organisztion of the production process lose their meaning, while the floors—which were never really valuable except for their generous capacity to host things—become graveyards of cables and wiring. These architectural skies emerge more clearly, drawing strength from their distance from the ground, from their detachment from what is happening on the ground.

UNDERGROUND. The foundations of this system are the prime witnesses to the abandonment taking place, colonized by water and vegetation as well as targeted excavations extracting infrastructural material and wiring. They are the protagonists of transformation. The geography of change—revealed by water stains, heaps of rubble, trenches and holes—is written in these spaces.

PILOT BUILDINGS AND ACTIVITIES. The recovery or reuse of this former production centre only seems feasible if it is interpreted as a city, not as a single building. The complexity of this structure and the value of the roofing compared to the vertical partitions do not allow its spaces to be fragmented, demanding the capitalization of its large volumes. The reactivation of this system should adopt the self-same strategies used to resuscitate parts of a city, not vast, all-embracing architectural solutions projected towards a single moment of realization, but the introduction of "pilot" activities and/or buildings whose role—even if just temporarily—is to attract new energy, which will in turn be able to reactivate this large space.

The current international debate on scenarios of abandonment delineates a trend of waiting rather than a prospective of global transformation and usage maximization, perspectives more characteristic of modernist thinking: "the princely progress of the human race"[24] is not of this time. As in the "spontaneous" regeneration of the former weapons production complex in Beijing, known today as Factory 798, where abandonment has led to its gradual "viral" occupation by artists. This complex is now a leading contemporary art centre that sprang up thanks to its state of abandonment. Moreover, when Factory 798 triggered a gentrification process throughout the surrounding urban area, the city administration's first thought was to pull down the old factory and build skyscrapers in its stead.

Today abandonment is the actor of transformation. A driver, if used as such, and not just a problem to be solved or eliminated. "Bail and switch" activities, chosen from activities compatible with the decommissioned facilities, would only require the introduction of small new working bodies, and could then make way for other, more structured activities with the economic potential necessary to revitalize the city's great sets.

[1] Peter Handke, *The Goalie's Anxiety at the Penalty Kick* (*Die Angst des Tormanns beim Elfmeter*, 1970), in Amos Leslie Willson, ed., *Contemporary German Stories* (London: Continuum International Publishing Group, 1998), p. 171.
[2] Cedric Price, *Re:CP* (Basel: Birkhäuser, 2003), p. 116.
[3] Jean Baudrillard, *Simulacres et simulation* (Paris: Galilée, 1981). English edition: *Simulacra and Simulation* (Ann Arbor: University of Michigan Press, 1994), p. 143.
[4] "Georges Perec is the writer whose long reflection on things has led to a novel of more than five hundred pages, *La vie mode d'emploi* [*Life: A User's Manual*] which appears to be one of the most radical examples of inclusive metaliterature. The structure of the book is provided by spatial, architectural data. Perec imagines a Parisian apartment whose façade is removed from the basement to the attic making all the rooms simultaneously visible. Next he goes on to narrate the lives and to describe the activities of the dwellers. The novel's metanarrative character consists in the fact that it is constructed as a puzzle made up of ninety-nine chapters within which multiple stories, classifications, directories, quotations, references interweave, branch off, overlap and develop

according to mechanisms of production sometimes self-evident, sometimes declared, sometimes respected, sometimes transgressed. The general effect of this immense and enigmatic work is that of reification pushed to extreme consequences. The 'life' alluded to in the title includes an infinity of things, different from one another, whose general sense seems justified by a common mania of collecting, classifying and preserving," Mario Perniola, *Il Sex appeal dell'inorganico* (Turin: Einaudi, 1994). English edition: *The Sex Appeal of the Inorganic* (London and New York: Continuum, 2004), p. 125.

[5] "What made the 1969 exhibit so interesting was its demonstration that an indexical sign could never be the exact, neutral, positive duplication of its referent. Not so much because most of the objects photographed were three-dimensional and, therefore, isomorphic with respect to their two-dimensional representations, but because the point of view of a photograph is precisely that, a point of view. In other words, it is supported by the exclusion structure of perspective and can never correspond to the point of view of the spectators whose eyes are in front of the object, in exactly the same point previously occupied by the lens," Yve-Alain Bois, *Martin Barré* (Paris: Flammarion, 1993), p. 70. Our translation.

[6] In his essay *La polvere nell'arte* Elio Grazioli examines waste as an element capable of bringing together matter and time, describing the "architecture=waste" equation proposed by Matta-Clark in the following terms: "The word 'anarchitecture' comes to us from Gordon Matta-Clark, an artist who knocked huge holes into the walls of abandoned buildings, thus making a lot of dust but, above all, treating architecture itself as dust," Elio Grazioli, *La polvere nell'arte* (Milan: Mondadori, 2004), p. 141. Our translation.

[7] Hal Foster, *Design and Crime (and Other Diatribes)* (London: Verso, 2002), p. 143.

[8] Kevin Lynch, *Wasting Away* (Michael Southworth ed.) (San Francisco: Sierra Club Books, 1990), p. 20.

[9] Jean Baudrillard, *Simulacra and Simulation*, p. 143.

[10] Kevin Lynch, p. 199.

[11] Haruki Murakami, *Dance Dance Dance* (New York: Vintage Books, 1995).

[12] Livio Sacchi, *Tokyo-to. Architettura e città* (Milan: Skira, 2004). Our translation.

[13] Jean-Luc Nancy, *L'intrus* (Paris: Editions Galilée, 2000). Our translation.

[14] Haruki Murakami.

[15] Ibid.

[16] Gianluca Bonaiuti and Alessandro Simoncini, *La catastrofe e il parassita. Scenari della transizione globale* (Milan: Mimesis, 2004), p. 32. Our translation.

[17] The prototype was built on the *Las Palmas* warehouse, Wilhelminakade 66–68, Kop van Zuid,

Rotterdam. The 85-square-metre building was erected between 2000 and 2001.

[18] Before being set up in Rotterdam, the exhibition *Parasites. The City of Small Things* had been hosted in Copenhagen (Architekturcentrum Gammel Dok, 5.8.2000), Oslo (Galerie ROM, 8.9.2000), London (Architectural Foundation, 10.12.2000), and Glasgow (The Lighthouse, 2.4.2001).

[19] Jennifer Allen, Hans Ibelings, and others, *Parasite Paradise. A Manifesto for Temporary Architecture and Flexible Urbanism* (Rotterdam: Nai Publishers, 2003).

[20] www.parasiteparadise.nl; www.beyondutrecht.nl.

[21] "The WiMBY! Project SchoolParasites won the 2004 Dutch Design Prize in the category 'Product for public space.' Onix, Christoph Seyfert and Barend designed three temporary school buildings—SchoolParasites—for WiMBY! Which were completed on 24 May 2004 in the Rotterdam district of Hoogvliet." www.skor.nl.

[22] Michel Serres, *Le Parasite* (Paris: Hachette, 1997). English edition: *The Parasite* (Minneapolis: University of Minnesota Press, 2007), p. 71.

[23] Vladimir Nabokov, *The Eye* (New York: Vintage, 1990), p. 51.

[24] Giacomo Leopardi, "The ginestra," in *The Poems of Giacomo Leopardi*, trans. Frederick Townsend (New York and London: G. P. Putman's Sons and The Knickerbocker Press, 1887).

Renato Bocchi

The Waste La
Fragments o
for a Hypoth
of Landscape

d-scape.

Thought

sis

as Palimpsest

April is the cruellest month, breeding
Lilacs out of the dead land, mixing
Memory and desire, stirring
Dull roots with spring rain.[1]

For the Venice Lagoon, or the Valli Grandi Veronesi—wastelands not because degraded but because marginalized, endangered lands not because attacked by development processes (though this could happen in a near future) but because for a long time excluded from the same processes—April is looming crueller than ever.

Grey storm clouds are gathering over these territories: a lagoon cancelled because flooded by the waters and returned to the open sea due to rising tides, or because reclaimed and returned to the mainland due to the need to bulwark against those same tides; marshlands wiped out by urban sprawl or by final abandonment and a return to their former swampy nature.[2]

What lilacs will ever blossom? What roots will stir with spring rain? How to reconcile memory with desire, past heritage with future plans?

Landscape lives in symbiosis with the living beings inhabiting it; without them it is mere nature, more or less wild, more or less unknown: *hic sunt leones*. Spring rain may stir the roots if places are populated and experienced, if heritage is not dispersed and if one has the courage to start over, to innovate.

The lagoon is full of "dead lands"—more or less abandoned islands, *sacche*, *barene*, ancient fortifications, docks and harbours, fishing ponds, huts and jetties, old and new grounds contending the sea. Maybe lilacs can bloom in these dead lands, infra-structuring new uses for these ancient sites.

What are the roots that clutch, what branches grow
Out of this stony rubbish? Son of man,
You cannot say, or guess, for you know only
A heap of broken images, where the sun beats,
And the dead tree gives no shelter, the cricket no relief,
And the dry stone no sound of water.

Today all that survives the wave of a development incapable of planning its outcome are scraps, fragments of landscape, heaps of broken images, the waste of a process that consumes but cannot devour anything, returning scrap upon scrap, waste upon waste.

Yet contemporary culture has learned to read and even romanticize these scraps, these fragments, not only for their material and economic value (the great theme of ecological recycling) but also for their formal evocative and emotional value (contemporary art is full of such approaches).[3]

Indeed, even our "emotions" can be "reifiable" fragments that could be used for a study on landscape.[4] The landscape of the future will probably be built on and with this waste.

Unreal City,
Under the brown fog of a winter dawn,

A crowd flowed over London Bridge, so many,
I had not thought death had undone so many,
Sighs, short and infrequent, were exhaled,
And each man fixed his eyes before his feet.

Unreal cities, surreal landscapes, swathed in dark fogs like those in Giovanni Battista Piranesi's *Carceri*, spatial mazes where we may still find obliterated identities along with new insights, archaeological landscapes like Piranesi's *formae urbis* proposing themselves as futuristic new scenarios…

Crowds of tourists happily splashing through the high water in the middle of depopulated wastelands: landscapes of ruins and ruins of landscapes. Although such doomsday scenarios are fortunately still distant enough—we hope—it is necessary to imagine which new landscapes may emerge from John Ruskin's *Stones of Venice*.[5]

This process bears strange similarities to the one described by John Soane in his remarkable text about his London house, imagined—in a very Piranesian exercise—as the site of a hypothetical archaeological ruin of classical Antiquity.[6]

Sweet Thames, run softly, till I end my song.
The river bears no empty bottles, sandwich papers,
Silk handkerchiefs, cardboard boxes, cigarette ends
Or other testimony of summer nights. The nymphs
are departed.

And their friends, the loitering heirs of City
directors;
Departed, have left no addresses.
…
Sweet Thames, run softly till I end my song,
Sweet Thames, run softly, for I speak not loud or
long.
But at my back in a cold blast I hear
The rattle of the bones, and chuckle spread from ear
to ear.
A rat crept softly through the vegetation
Dragging its slimy belly on the bank
While I was fishing in the dull canal
On a winter evening round behind the gashouse
Musing upon the king my brother's wreck
And on the king my father's death before him.

The waters may be salvific if they run softly, if they become the connective tissue of our sailing, characterizing the lagoon for centuries as well as the hydrographic network that made the Bassa Veronese marshes habitable.

In water is life, not just death by water. Each archipelago lives thanks to the water that connects it. The isolation of islands can be contrasted through their aggregation and water is an essential connective element. For archipelagos water is part of a vital relationship.

Once again the water can be strategic for the regeneration of the earth; *water*scapes may restore the

identity of *land*scapes. Maybe the lagoon can still teach us this if we are capable of listening to it.[7]

> At the violet hour, when the eyes and back
> Turn upward from the desk, when the human engine
>   waits
>   Like a taxi throbbing waiting,
> I Tiresias, though blind, throbbing between two lives,
> Old man with wrinkled female breasts, can see
> At the violet hour, the evening hour that strives
> Homeward, and brings the sailor home from sea,
> The typist home at teatime, clears her breakfast, lights
>   Her stove, and lays out food in tins.

At the violet hour bringing sailors home, we might rediscover a lagoon not only unlike its former self but unlike its present self: a landscape of landscapes that reassembles in a new light. The palimpsests live because they are preserved, deleted and re-written, keeping track of what was there and revealing new signs, in a completely different light.[8] And maybe even the surviving inhabitants of the lagoons can be reconsidered, at the violet hour, at tea time, as part of those landscapes.

As in a video by Bill Viola, the violet hour marks the passing of time, constructing ever-changing landscapes with its dynamic scrolling.

As in an installation by Claudio Parmiggiani, the violet hour creates "places where the protagonists are just light and shadow,"[9] as in his *Delocazioni*, "the visual mat-

ter is formed in the *blown*, atmospheric, exhaled movement of the particles of combustion emitted by the fire."[10]

Not a desert or a ruin, indeed, but a transfigured landscape, capable of giving new meanings even to the remains of the past: "… when the atmosphere takes shape… as in the fog, in the dusk, or in the shade of things."[11]

> "This music crept by me upon the waters"
> And along the Strand, up Queen Victoria Street.
>   O City city, I can sometimes hear
> Beside a public bar in Lower Thames Street,
>   The pleasant whining of a mandoline
>   And a clatter and a chatter from within
> Where fishmen lounge at noon: where the walls
>   Of Magnus Martyr hold
> Inexplicable splendour of Ionian white and gold.
>   The river sweats
>   Oil and tar
>   The barges drift
>   With the turning tide
>   Red sails
>   Wide
> To leeward, swing on the heavy spar.
>   The barges wash
>   Drifting logs
>   Down Greenwich reach
>   Past the Isle of Dogs.

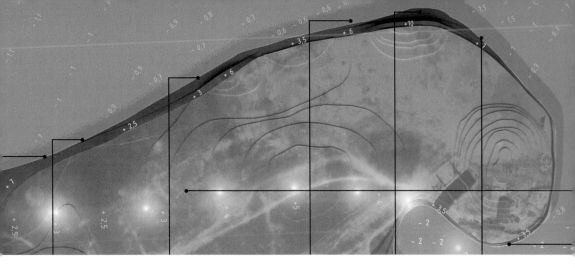

Cities, canals, stagnant waters—in both the Lagoon and the Valli Grandi—are still the key features of the landscape, even of the future one, in an unstable equilibrium, in a process obviously requiring continuous adjustments but accommodating vital processes.

Today the city and the lagoon, the city and the marshlands, are distant realities turning their backs on each other, based on conflicting alternative physical and life laws. Tomorrow reality could, should, consider recomposing them in a new unit. Not a city invading the lagoon or marshlands, nor water invading and eroding the city. We need to conceive of a more complementary and integrated body, a landscape of different fragments, each with its "plural" identity, a landscape-city, a city of water, capable of speaking a new language as well as of interpreting changing and liquid movements and flows of life.

Not a world anchored fast, nor a world in equilibrium, not a world embalmed but a world open to change, as mobile as the water, ready to reflect the lights and colours of every hour of the day and night, ready to welcome people, all kinds of people, provided they are willing to plunge into that kaleidoscope of colour and light rather than contemplating it from afar.[12]

> Phlebas the Phoenician, a fortnight dead,
> Forgot the cry of gulls, and the deep sea swell
> And the profit and loss.
> A current under sea
> Picked his bones in whispers. As he rose and fell

> He passes the stages of his age and youth
> Entering the whirlpool.
> Gentile or Jew
> O you who turn the wheel and look windward,
> Consider Phlebas, who was once handsome and
> tall as you.

Death by water. For Venice a fate foretold. As for the Valli Veronesi.

Weighing up the profits and losses is not so hard, all things considered. Embalming could be considered a profitable scenario, after all. As could abandonment: "Consider Phlebas, who was once handsome." However, we'd rather consider this a final solution only. One evoking the charm of the sublime, as in Thomas Mann's *Death in Venice*.

Considering the "bones in whispers" as materials for a work—albeit a *Merzbau* of fragments with its own innovative programme—seems a more credible and more hopeful goal.[13]

> After the torchlight red on sweaty faces
> After the frosty silence in the gardens
> After the agony in stony places
> The shouting and the crying
> Prison and palace and reverberation
> Of thunder of spring over distant mountains
> He who was living is now dead
> We who were living are now dying

With a little patience
Here is no water but only rock
Rock and no water and the sandy road
The road winding above among the mountains
Which are mountains of rock without water
If there were water we should stop and drink
Amongst the rock one cannot stop or think
...
Unreal
A woman drew her long black hair out tight
And fiddled whisper music on those strings
And bats with baby faces in the violet light
Whistled, and beat their wings
And crawled head downward down a blackened wall
And upside down in air were towers
Tolling reminiscent bells, that kept the hours
And voices singing out of empty cisterns and
exhausted wells.

What if death were "by ground"? No more water, just ground, not necessarily bleak?

Even this scenario is not entirely unlikely. The Dutch *polders*, behind their high dams, are not so different.[14] It would be a curious twist of fate for Venice to be a new Amsterdam. After all Chioggia already is to some extent.

As are the Valli Veronesi, attached to their *città diffusa veneta*, that urban sprawl characterizing the Veneto, "archmetropolitanized."

Instead of the sublime, the prosaic picture of metropolitan growth: Mestre triumphant, the American city *par excellence*, and Venice reduced to historic centre. No more water, or maybe just sweet water, not clear and fresh. The victory of the hinterland.

London Bridge is falling down falling down falling
down
Poi s'ascose nel foco che gli affina
Quando fiam uti chelidon—O swallow swallow
Le Prince d'Aquitaine à la tour abolie
These fragments I have shored against my ruins
Why then Ile fit you. Hieronymo's mad againe.
Datta. Dayadhvam. Damyata.
Shantih shantih shantih

"These fragments I have shored against my ruins." This is the solution proposed by T. S. Eliot, accepting all the cruelty of an April that may be bleak but still full of promise.

The discards of the local growth and transformation process of the territory might be—by analogy with the method and poetics suggested by Eliot—fragments of a speech-landscape to be overwritten/drawn upon the space-time of places that now seem to have been rejected.

Eliot's *The Waste Land* seems to suggest that all we can do is design a process (encompassing every possible variability and adaptability) capable of building (time-space) relationships between those waste fragments: a dada *Merzbau à la* Kurt Schwitters or an El Lissitsky Constructivist *Proun*, rather than a Cubist painting adopting a compositional method rather than a de-compositional one and carefully considering and incorporating *becoming* and, therefore, temporal dynamics or *change*, not so much in its "analytical" function but in terms of its "projecting" function.[15]

But Eliot's method seems to warn us that to do this it is not enough to control the process of re-composition and processing: we must set ourselves a goal of final order. We must rediscover the "mythical method," transferring even moods and emotions to the reality of the senses—i.e. to the landscape—and chasing the myth.[16]

"To use the words of Claude Lévi-Strauss: 'Savage thought does not distinguish the moment of observation and that of interpretation' […]. The adoption of the mythical system allows Eliot to create a poetic programme aimed at bridging the gap between statements of facts and judgements of value in order to establish in its place a form of communication and perception in which the two phases are indistinguishable," writes Franco Moretti about *The Waste Land*. "The first chapter of the *Savage Mind* is illuminating in this respect, and the analogy between mythical construction and *bricolage* can reasonably be extended to *The Waste Land*. Like the *bricoleur*, Eliot draws some elements (typically sentences or verses) from various kinds of organized sets, choosing precisely those elements that are capable of performing a new function—more or less dis-

tant from the original—in the new structure that is *The Waste Land*."[17]

"The characteristic feature of mythical thought, as of *bricolage* on the practical plane," wrote Lévi-Strauss, "is that it builds up structured sets, not directly with other structured sets but by using the remains and debris of events […] fossilized evidence of the history of an individual or a society."[18]

"The fragment," ends Moretti, "becomes a function: what is striking is not its being divorced and mutilated, but the fact that it has a clearly defined significance and role, and effectively contributes to building a new and organized whole."

Thus we must just collect the "fragments shored against the ruins," like Robert Smithson in his wanderings among the "monuments" of Passaic in order to find the roots that take hold, even when travelling in the *junkspace* of Postmodernity.[19] So maybe lilacs can still blossom in these wastelands.

Building—more than a tale—a (hypertextual) montage of things and pictures capable of narrating in a simultaneous and continuously evolving spatial framework rather than in a chronological sequence; a palimpsest that is constantly erased and rewritten, but where traces remain to build a continuum: traces of culture, the geo-archaeological layers that are our heritage.

Perhaps this is the myth constructed by the accumulation of erudite culture and material culture, which is in Eliot the accumulation of Eastern and Western lit-

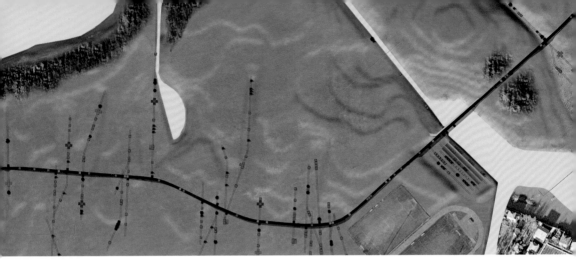

erary culture mixed with everyday life, something like that myth that Piranesi pursued by drawing antiquities to construct scenes that appear like incredible forerunners of modern life.

Just as it is interesting to juxtapose Eliot's poetry with anthropological thought (not just of Lévi-Strauss, but even of James G. Frazer and his *Golden Bough*), so can landscape design be compared to landscape anthropology, as the geographer Eugenio Turri has so brilliantly done—also dealing specifically with the Venetian Lagoon.[20]

"Meanwhile, we must remember that both *The Waste Land* and *The Golden Bough*," points out Fabio Dei, "are intertextual works: i.e. they are entirely constructed as a montage of pieces or fragments of other texts, extracted from their original cultural context and authorship, and placed in a new order. Eliot's quotations range from the Bible to the classical myths, from Dante to Shakespeare, from St. Augustine to the Upanishads. Like Frazer, he builds up his own discursive authority by commanding an entire universe of texts, extraordinarily far-reaching in terms of both space and time [...]. Moreover, the scraps of texts composing the work cover very different periods and cultures, deliberately dissolving any semblance of unitary context [...]. All that keeps this together is a general narrative structure, which seems to be capable of incorporating the different contexts: the ritualistic interpretation of the legend of the Holy Grail that Eliot takes from Weston.

Namely, a tale of a journey and a search—the same metaphors underpinning the *Golden Bough*."[21]

"In using the myth, in manipulating a continuous parallel between contemporaneity and antiquity," Eliot himself wrote, commenting on the Joyce's *Ulysses*, "Mr. Joyce is pursuing a method which others must pursue after him [...]. It is simply a way of controlling, of ordering, of giving a shape and a significance to the immense panorama of futility and anarchy which is contemporary history [...]. Psychology, ethnology, and *The Golden Bough* have concurred to make possible what was impossible even a few years ago. Instead of narrative method, we may now use the mythical method. It is, I seriously believe, a step toward making the modern world possible for art."[22]

"Yet the mythical method," concludes Fabio Dei, "does not limit itself to dissolving the traditional order of history, transforming it into a chaotic mass of unrelated fragments. Its aim is to bring about the emergence of a new order from these fragments. *Shall I at least set my lands in order?* is the question that the Fisher King, the narrator of *The Waste Land*, asks himself in its last lines (*I sat upon the shore / Fishing, with the arid plain behind me / Shall I at least set my lands in order?*, vv. 423–25). This is the crucial question that Eliot asks. The Search to which the poem alludes appears as a search for order. But this new order must emerge from the ruins of the former one, which must then be traced back, on a journey towards the wellsprings of man's

moral identity. Thus the same imagery and the same geological 'method' that we saw at work in Frazer and Freud reappear in Eliot."[23]

Though landscape design is undeniably also a journey and a narrative project, it is possibly even more so—especially in the context of fragments and ruins like the ones under discussion—a project of hypertextual narration, similar to the one above, whose ultimate goal alludes to a new order, however complex.[24]

So this is the landscape of the lagoon, a country at once archaic and futuristic. This is also the landscape of the Valli Grandi Veronesi.

Landscapes where the banality of this present time has not yet made premium on the past and future, where peripheralization is not about the "periferia diffusa" (suburban sprawl) described by Vitaliano Trevisan,[25] but about a process where abandonment and exclusion have prevailed over economic and settlement growth.

Territories of a possible future, therefore, where it is still possible to write without having to erase too much. Primarily using the white spaces and then perhaps other more material scraps.

A less soaring *Merzbau*, in whose interstices the first, second and third landscapes[26] can continue to flourish, *breeding lilacs out of the dead land*.

Perhaps death is not by water, then. Maybe it is water that will save us, as when we fled Attila's hordes. Surviving on the edges, building the new world?

[1] Thomas Stearns Eliot, *The Waste Land* (New York: Boni & Liveright, 1922).

[2] "The myth of the Waste Land was born among nomad populations or in primitive farming settlements that had a relationship of mere subsistence with the land. The enigma of a physical nature subject to seasonal cycles or cataclysmic events is resolved by the epiphany of the will of a higher being that has become hostile or incapable of guaranteeing the constant production of the land," Mario Melchionda, "Introduzione," in Thomas Stearns Eliot, *The Waste Land* (Milan: Mursia, 1976), pp. 18–19.

[3] See, among many studies on the topic, Lea Vergine, *When Trash Becomes Art: Trash Rubbish Mongo* (Milan: Skira, 2007).

[4] T. S. Eliot wrote in *Hamlet and his Problems: The Sacred Wood* (London: Methuen & Co., 1920): "The only way of expressing emotion in the form of art is by finding an 'objective correlative'; in other words, a set of objects, a situation, a chain of events which shall be the formula of that *particular* emotion; such that when the external facts, which must terminate in sensory experience, are given, the emotion is immediately evoked." He compares the "objective correlative" to a metaphor which "reifies" itself. I believe that this concept perfectly fits the theme of landscape and the possible "reification" that it proposes for the intangible emotions or perceptions of its user.

[5] A recent intelligent recycling of Ruskin's *Stones of Venice*—in an effective comparison with the surprising "popular" photographic archive of Alvio Gavagnin on the present Venetian City of Society—is offered by Wolfgang Scheppe, ed., in his *Done. Book. Picturing the City of Society* (Ostfildern: Hatje Cantz, 2010).

[6] "A similar aesthetic of hybridization, fragmentation, accumulation and recomposition compels John Soane to design, build, describe his home, which perhaps is really his Capriccio [...]. Henry James paid a visit to Sir John Soane and his house in No. 13 has become the cornerstone of a theory of modern fiction," Caroline Patey, "A zonzo: nel tempo e nel testo," in John Soane, *Per una storia della mia casa* (Palermo: Sellerio, 2010), original title: *Crude Hints towards an History of My House*, pp. 13–31.

[7] "Without understanding the importance of water as a connective space, for Venice and for its lagoon, we cannot easily understand the particular quality of life in Venice [...]. The idea of a lagoon park takes on a fundamental value, in my view, precisely if it involves the objective of reunifying and rebalancing the lagoon and the city, reinforcing the connective potential of water spaces," Renato Bocchi, "The Venice Lagoon: Survival Paradigm," in *2G Dossier, 2G Competition. Venice Lagoon Park*, Barcelona, 2008, pp. 90–92. Concerning the fundamental value of water for the urban settlement, I like to mention Paolo Sica's words: "Of the four elements that ancient populations considered the foundation of the cosmos, water resembles the earth, because like the earth it is subject to the force of gravity. Yet unlike the earth (i.e. buildings and cities), which is fixed and heavy by nature, water is mobile. This opposition to the mineral hardness of the built city makes water a vehicle of imagery. Why imagery? The river runs toward an unknown goal (or an invisible one), nothing keeps it inside the city walls. While calm waters have the power to duplicate objects, recreating them in a reverse mirror dimension that is inaccessible," Paolo Sica, "Firenze, città e fiume," in *La Città e il Fiume, Arch/Under*

or design finite forms for the project or for the safeguarding of the landscape: they will be short-lived. We need to be capable of designing process routes comprising instability, variability, and even transience. In this sense, landscape design is absolutely modern, because it takes into account the indefiniteness, instability, and extreme subjective diversity characterizing the world we live in. The more it is able to adapt and reinterpret the constantly changing world, the more effective and lasting it will be," abstract from "Point 11" by Renato Bocchi, in Juan Manuel Palerm Salazar, ed., *Manifiesto por el proyecto de paisaje europeo* (Las Palmas: Observatorio del Paisaje, Gobierno de Canarias, 2011).

[13] "Sacca San Mattia is a place apart, without history, without form, without life, or perhaps a realm of possible biological diversities like many other *terrains vagues*, a place stolen from the sea and produced by the refuse of the city and the lagoon itself [...]. Perhaps it is a possible machine for virtuous recycling of the waste of a crocodile-civilisation that devours its landscape-world and then cries over its loss. Perhaps it can also be the landing strip for a most virtuous touristic exploration of the lagoon

(Milan: Electa, 1987), p. 181, quoted in Renato Bocchi, "Fiume e città: così lontani così vicini," *Archi* 1 (2011), pp. 13–18. Two interesting social-artistic experiments on the role of water in the Venetian lagoon are: Lucy+Jorge Orta, *Drinkwater* (Venice: Fondazione Bevilacqua La Masa, 2005), and Marjetica Potrc, *Rainwater Harvesting* (Venice: Fondazione Bevilacqua La Masa, 2010). See for this: Angela Vettese, "Quattro riletture di Venezia", in Alberto Bertagna, ed., *Paesaggi fatti ad arte* (Macerata: Quodlibet, 2010), pp. 47–54.

[8] "We consider the landscape a territorial palimpsest where local communities record their human history. The palimpsest-landscape is therefore a landscape aspiring to being a work of continuous re-writing while maintaining an overall 'personality' or making sure that every sign that is added or removed works together to give meaning to the new figure of the whole," Renato Bocchi, *Arcipelaghi del rifiuto: dalla laguna di Venezia alle Valli Grandi Veronesi*, in Annalisa Calcagno Maniglio, ed., *Progetti di paesaggio per i luoghi rifiutati* (Rome: Gangemi, 2010), pp. 83–88.

[9] *Claudio Parmiggiani, Luce, luce, luce*, exhibition catalogue (Toulon: Hôtel des Arts, 1999), p. 8.

[10] Georges Didi-Huberman, *Sculture d'ombra aria polvere impronte fantasmi* (Milan: Electa, 2009), p. 13.

[11] Ibid., p. 42.

[12] "The dimension of moving perception defines landscapes both in their emotional and narrative features, and allows changeable and multiple interpretations of them. Hence the importance, even in landscape design, of the dynamic dimension, of the narrative construction or the meaningful montage of assembled relationships between users (in movement) and physical, constituent elements of those particular places. In addition, the landscape itself is also mutable, because the time factor—the changing of light during the day, the changing of climate and seasons during the year—are constantly changing the character of the landscape, and therefore also the experience. This emphasizes the process of change attributable to the government of landscape transformations, associated with its planning and maintenance over time. It is a project for a system of spatial, physical, topological relationships that change over time and whose variability we should expect, or at least take into account. It is useless therefore to seek

park," Renato Bocchi, "The Venice Lagoon: Survival Paradigm."

[14] "If we need to protect Venice from exceptional high waters (using as an order of magnitude events where the tide exceeds +1.50 metres above the mean sea-level) it is our duty to point out that no check can be carried out without interrupting the flow at the inlets: with fixed or mobile works [...]. On this point all models and evaluations that are only minimally judicious are in agreement," Andrea Rinaldo, *Il governo dell'acqua. Ambiente naturale e ambiente costruito* (Venice: Marsilio, 2009), p. 180. If the dams were fixed rather than mobile, it is quite obvious even to a layman like myself that the lagoon would come to resemble a Dutch polder.

[15] "The language with which the everyday world is written is like a patchwork of languages, like a graffiti-covered wall full of writing on top of each other, a palimpsest whose parchment was scraped clean and rewritten several times, a collage by Schwitters, a layering of alphabets, heterogenous quotations, slang terms, snappy characters as they appear on the screen of a computer," Italo Calvino, "Ipotesi di descrizione di un paesaggio," in Various Authors, *Esplorazioni della via Emilia* (Milan: Feltrinelli, 1986).

[16] See footnote 2. In this sense, as noted by Enzo Paci in *Esistenza ed immagine* (Milan: Tarantola, 1947), "between the poetry of Eliot and his metaphysical needs a myth interposes itself." "A myth," explains Roberto Sanesi, "which itself acts as a connective tissue for all contradictions, in a syncretistic and open vision. As happens in James Joyce, and Eliot was perfectly aware of this. So much so that from 1923 he feels the function of the mythical world is to monitor, filter, give shape and significance to the immense panorama of futility and anarchy which is contemporary history," Roberto Sanesi, "Eliot, crisi e progetto," in T. S. Eliot, *Opere* (Milan: Bompiani, 1986), p. XII.

[17] Franco Moretti, "Dalla Terra desolata al paradiso artificiale," *Calibano* 5 (1980).

[18] See Claude Lévi-Strauss, *La Pensée sauvage* (Paris: Plon, 1962). English edition: *The Savage Mind* (Chicago: University of Chicago Press, 1966), pp. 21–22.

[19] "That zero panorama seemed to contain *ruins in reverse*, that is—all the new construction that would eventually be built. This is the opposite of the 'romantic ruin' because the buildings don't *fall* into ruin *after* they are built but rather *rise* into ruin *before* they are built. This anti-romantic *mise en scène* suggests the discredited idea of *time* and many other 'out-of-date' things. But the suburbs exist without a rational past and without the 'big events' of history. Oh, maybe there are a few statues, a legend and a couple of curios, but no past—just what passes for a future [...]. Passaic seems full of 'holes' compared to New York City, which seems tightly packed and solid, and those holes in a sense are the monumental vacancies that define, without trying, the memory-traces of an abandoned set of futures. Such futures are found in grade-B utopian films, and then imitated by the suburbanite [...]. Time turns metaphors into things, and stacks them up in cold rooms, or places them in the celestial playgrounds of the suburbs," Robert Smithson, "The Monuments of Passaic: Has Passaic Replaced Rome as the Eternal City?," *Artforum* (New York, December 1967).

[20] See Eugenio Turri, *Antropologia del paesaggio* (Venice: Marsilio, 2008, new edition), and Giovanni Caniato, Eugenio Turri, Michele Zanetti, eds., *La Laguna di Venezia* (Verona: Cierre, 1995).

[21] Fabio Dei, *Metodo mitico e comparazione antropologica. Frazer e The Golden Bough cent'anni dopo*;

unpublished in Italian, this text
was originally presented at the
conference "Antropología: Horizontes
comparativos," Granada, C.I.E. *Ángel
Ganivet*, 24–27 May 2000; then
published in Spanish in Carmelo Lisón
Tolosana, ed., *Antropología: Horizontes
comparativos* (Granada: Universidad
de Granada, 2001), pp. 39–66.
The essay takes up some themes
developed more fully in Fabio Dei,
*La discesa agli inferi. James G. Frazer
e la cultura del Novecento*
(Lecce: Argo, 1998).
[22] See "*Ulysses*, Order and Myth,"
The Dial 75 (November 1923), then
Frank Kermode, ed., *Selected Prose
of T. S. Eliot* (London: Faber
and Faber, 1975), p. 483.
[23] Fabio Dei, *Metodo mitico*.
[24] "The programme of a landscape
project resembles a storyboard
or a script for a play or a film more
than an architectural project [...].
The conceptual, narrative,
interpretative base plays a fundamental
role in bringing to life the inventive
process (of discovery and invention),
and then the creative process [...].
I have long been fascinated by the idea
of landscape as a palimpsest layered
with signs, traces, memories, writings
and of a project as the words
overwriting that palimpsest:
an interpretative overwriting with its

own internal logic, capable of giving
a relational reading of things
and the spaces between things that
this palimpsest can reveal [...].
So maybe Ariosto's *Orlando Furioso*
with its narrative 'hypertextual'
structure and its evocation of fantastic
pictures, can be the trace, the guiding
idea, the script, of a landscape design
project," Renato Bocchi, "Le strutture
narrative e il progetto del paesaggio,"
in Corrado Olmi, ed., *Il Parco
dell'Ariosto e del Boiardo* (Macerata:
Quodlibet, 2010), pp. 41–50.
[25] "You have the impression of moving
or living in a *periferia diffusa*,
a suburban sprawl, more than a *città
diffusa* (urban sprawl). In fact,
contemporary architecture seems
to exclusively produce suburbs, at least
here—I mean in Italy and the Veneto
in particular [...]. *Periferia diffusa*
is a very different concept to *città
diffusa*, less reassuring, less elegant
[...]. It is clear to me, and it seems
logical, that it is a suburb rather than
a city, and it seems no less clear
and logical that it is widespread
and continues to spread," Vitaliano
Trevisan, *Tristissimi giardini*
(Rome-Bari: Laterza, 2010),
pp. 13–15.
[26] The reference is obviously to Gilles
Clément, *Manifeste du tiers paysage*
(Paris: Sujet/Objet, 2004).

Giovanni Corbellini

Resid

uals

Towards the end of the last century, the Dutch architecture firm MVRDV put forward
    an experimental project that comprised/compressed a population of 200 million
    inhabitants into a self-sufficient metropolis. All the activities necessary for its
    sustenance (energy production, food, goods and services, housing, education
    and leisure, transport and waste disposal, storage infrastructures...) had to be
    contained in a square measuring 400 by 400 kilometres. The three-dimensional
    simulations of *Metacity Datatown*[1] reveal the drastic consequences of our life style,
    even when tempered by the application of cutting-edge technologies. The most
    striking quantitative output of these simulations are the waste mountains on the
    edges of the hyper-dense urban fabric looming tens of times higher than the

skyscrapers. A few years later, towering waste heaps with the same parabolic profiles imagined by MVRDV can be seen cluttering up every corner of the future earth, now a giant dump abandoned by all forms of life and home to *Wall-E*,[2] a small trash-compactor robot and hero of one of the latest successes in computer animation.

Waste bursting onto the scene of a kid's film marks its definitive entry into the collective consciousness as a plausible and menacingly imminent scenario, borne out by several real events and their narrative interpretations. At the time the *Mobro 4000* incident may have seemed like an isolated event. But the huge barge that left New York in March 1987 with over three thousand tonnes of the city's trash, wandering from port to port and reaching Belize before turning back for its destination where its load was incinerated in Brooklyn seven months later, was just an early warning. The following year the National Oceanic and Atmospheric Administration of the United States published a paper predicting the formation of an accumulation of debris that soon hit the headlines as the Pacific Trash Vortex, approximately 100 million tonnes of plastic particulate suspended in the sea north of Hawai and east of Japan whose surface area is now estimated at between 1 and 15 million square kilometres. Closer to home, the Neapolitan waste management crisis has been festering since 1994, the year of the first administration by an external commissioner. In 2001 thousands of tonnes of waste were sent daily to other Italian regions and even to Germany, where incineration cost less than in-situ disposal of the waste bales or *ecoballe*, an Italian neologism meaning "eco-bales/balls" that has gradually acquired increasing significance.[3] Underworld influences, social disintegration, inefficiency and political interests all come together in the ongoing Neapolitan emergency which regularly causes rotting piles of garbage to spill over into the city centre, the media and uncustomary international coverage (thanks also to web tools like Google Maps Street View). It is hardly surprising then that two of the most important novels of recent years focus on waste. Don DeLillo makes it the key theme of *Underworld*[4] where constant symbolical and tangible references to the concealed, the removed, are set into motion by the leading character, a waste management executive. And in *Infinite Jest*,[5] David Foster Wallace imagines that much of the north-eastern United States has become a huge inaccessible waste dump, the "Great Concavity," comprising territory scarred by toxic waste and industrial processes and now a no man's land where the debris of the entire nation can be dumped.

It seems that the development model that Francis Fukuyama holds responsible for the *End of history*[6] will really end up bringing it about, not so much and not merely as a definitive form of political and economic rule based on the secularization of the free market but in far wider-reaching and dramatically terminal ways. In fact, we outstripped our planet's ability to regenerate its resources back in the 1980s and it would now take two earths to support our standards of living. As various emerging countries experience the diffusion of levels of affluence aspiring to Western standards, in the first world (the main culprit for this situation with an ecological footprint between 5 and 6 for Europeans, Australians and Japanese, 10 for North Americans and 12[7] for the Emirates) people are increasingly asking themselves how to reduce externalities, culminating in the radical "zero emission" option. Among the leading proponents of drastically reducing environmental impact are William McDonough, American architect, and Michael Braungart, German chemist and green activist. Together they wrote *Cradle to Cradle*,[8] an analysis of current conditions, proposals and strategies challenging both the ingrained prejudices of turbocapitalist thought as well as those of its ecological counterparts. They call into question the effectiveness of recycling that seems to condemn various materials to reincarnation as inferior life forms. In fact, the impurities that accumulate every time materials are reintroduced into the production cycle reduce performance levels, meaning that the high strength steel used in cars is reused in the construction sector, virgin paper becomes cardboard and similar fates await plastic and aluminium. According to the two authors these energy-intensive downcycling processes are not without risks for health. After examining the possibility of producing their book as a technical system, McDonough and Braungart concluded that the differences between recycled and virgin cellulose paper are not that great and that the more "blandly ecological" solution might prove more dangerous in the long run.[9] They decided to print the original edition on a washable polymer stock that could be recycled—together with the ink—virtually endlessly, a practical example of how to rethink the way things are made. We need to develop an integrated approach to the design of goods and services as well as to their production and consumption models in order to cancel their impact or invert them positively, giving back to the environment more than we have taken away. Though fascinating, this concept relies on a substantially positivist belief in design and its capacity to imitate the regenerative complexity of natural ecosystems which are seen as balanced, intrinsically good "machines" existing in virtual isolation from each other and, above all, from the artificial world and its underlying logic. Although sensitive to a sustainability embracing both social and market considerations, the examples of virtuous design described in the essay are more Lamarckian than Darwinian in their vision of nature, viewing interactions between species in terms of collaborative aims rather than

as fierce, unpredictable, dynamic and selective conflicts. From this point of view, the "ecoefficient" project risks suffering from the same contradictions that undermined the effectiveness of the original modern project, which foundered in the impossibility of managing complex systems and their growing uncertainty. What is more, the fact that biological function models are infinitely more complicated and sophisticated than the Taylorism adopted by Le Corbusier and Gropius as an example leads to the exponential growth of the possible side effects inevitably linked to "good intentions."

Even the more politically correct proposals sold as eco-friendly are affected by the same syndrome of vertical control as the manifestos of naïve functionalism with zero impact once again translating into closed systems, designed to be impermeable to all kinds of unforeseen behaviour or event. The "sustainable" cities springing up in the Arabian deserts are walled cities, limited in time and space, strongly motivated by the desire to keep all that is uncertain beyond their boundaries. Significantly Norman Foster's Masdar project in Abu Dhabi, the Oma Rak Gateway City and Dubai Waterfront City all share the same self-enclosed square plan where the entrance controls typical of gated communities take on the symbolic, military, atopical dimension of the Roman *castrum*.[10] The energy self-sufficiency of these projects distracts our attention from the blatant contradictions lying at their heart.

The potential residents presumably belong to the international jet-set and are thus likely to have particularly large ecological footprints.[11] The fact that they will travel by plane to these second and third homes owing their existence to absence of fiscal pressure is unlikely to improve matters. Masdar perfectly reproduces the mean cross-section of the population in Emirate countries with 70% of its work force made up of non-residents[12] who are truly second-class citizens living out "wasted lives"[13] in separate locations from which they can be immediately expelled if they lose their jobs. (Travellers returning from Dubai during the height of the financial crisis described how thousands of hire cars had been abandoned at the airport by Palestinian, Filipino, Indian, etc. workers who had lost their permits of stay along with their jobs.)

The authoritarian urges and social cynicism so closely associated with this corner of the world and the other financial paradises come together with intrinsic technological limits. According to the head of Arup Energy, "sustainable" arm of the famous international engineering firm, as things stand today it is impossible to conceive of a zero-emission urban structure with a population of over one hundred thousand inhabitants (Masdar is due to reach fifty thousand by 2020). This limit concerns cities built from scratch and does not apply to refurbishments or retrofitted mature cities.[14] It would be interesting to discover to what extent "grey energy" contributes to the total, that is, whether the greater initial investment required attaining the requested outcome is effectively recovered during the project life-cycle... In any case, the unique situation in the Emirates provides us with the ideal terrain to freely test the extreme consequences of closed-cycle systems and of the various scenarios linked to waste elimination, in technical terms and, above all, in ideological terms. In fact, the general perception of green aims as being intrinsically "good" has caused them to be taken up by political forces all over the world (at least in terms of marketing, thus leading to the progressive disappearance of the parties identifying with this theme). Leaving aside for the moment the attempts to put them into practice, the global acceptance of such themes triggers and feeds forms of simplification that are gradually transforming ecology from a science of complex dynamic interrelations into the dominant ideology of global capitalism. According to Slavoj Žižek the driving force behind this metamorphosis is fear, which is just as effective in this area as the security syndrome that causes the wealthy classes to wall themselves up in ever more heavily guarded confines. Fear of an environmental catastrophe, of the finite nature of our planet and its resources have led to its definitive sacralization as "something that should not be unveiled totally, that should and will forever remain a Mystery, a power we should trust, not dominate."[15] The "ecology of fear" has tended to replace religion, retrieving its role as undiscussed authority and instrument of social control, with all its myths, rituals and behaviours. And although it asks us to make radical changes in our life styles, it is at the same time underpinned by a deep reluctance to admit effective change, a refusal of every form of development or progress.

Opposing this vision of a sacred nature whose harmony is threatened by humankind is an anthropocentric idea seeing the continuous unpredictable changes in natural

ecosystems responsible for numerous instances of large-scale extinction in the past as a threat for the survival of humankind. The idea that the earth's evolution can be frozen in an ideal situation by means of constant measures capable of maintaining its equilibrium leads to a similar idea of homeostatic equilibrium. In *KM3*[16] MVRDV explores the consequences of extending zero-balance management to the entire planet—not just for emissions but for the entire production cycle—focusing as usual on quantities and the planning consequences linked to their integrated management. Here the hoped-for aim of guaranteeing future generations a future is accompanied by the disquieting risk of producing a truly total institution whose control over nature, not just human nature, would be more intrusive than

the free-market model it wishes to replace (an institution that MVRDV themselves seem to suggest we should escape, ending their book with a proposal for a project to colonize interplanetary space...).

Leaving aside the same considerations advanced for *Cradle to Cradle* concerning the feasibility of bringing about such extensive control of a hugely complex and intrinsically unstable system, the power of the figures emerging from the research carried out by MVRDV reveals the tragic vitality of the current production-consumption spiral. In the short term, this is a situation that we cannot avoid dealing with, especially in the specific field of architecture. "Junkspace will be our tomb. Half of mankind pollutes to produce, the other pollutes to consume," writes Rem Koolhaas in one of his most apocalyptic and visionary essays,[17] extending the pervasive condition of waste to the whole of contemporary spatial production. According to Koolhaas, regardless of their quality and meaning, the sum of the single architectural actions leads to an entropic proliferation defying any attempt at hierarchy or composition. "More and more is more"[18] is the umpteenth (per)version of the minimalist motto of Mies subjected to an additive obsession revealing paradoxical potential in its excessive dimensions: "Junkspace seems an aberration, but it is essence, the main thing."[19] Reading between the lines of a terrifying analysis of real economic processes and their consequences, we can identify the possibility of a perceptive dislocation, an inversion of judgement where the selective evaluation of waste and its real consequences connects to similar intuitions developed in the fields of psychoanalysis, philosophy and art. We could even develop a line of thought originating with Freud and his reflections on the expression *Heimlich*, or familiar, and, above all, on its changing meaning encompassing reassuring domesticity along with more obscure disturbing threats.[20] According to the great Viennese master, the idea of familiarity is transformed into a disquieting threatening sensation by the re-emergence of what has been removed. When the eliminated, the refused, attains a certain critical mass, by-product becomes protagonist, a driver for interpretation and innovation. This condition was explored to the extreme by Georges Bataille whose obsessive immersion in degradation, corruption and "base materialism" transforms the "unformed" into an indispensible operative category for the understanding of contemporary thought and, above all, of numerous art forms.[21] The elevation of everyday objects to works of art explored by Marcel Duchamp with his ready-mades opens the door to a series of low/high inversions emblematically represented by his overturning, both literally and conceptually, of a urinal, significantly transformed by the French artist into a "fountain." This gave rise to a series of lines of research linked to subtraction (Yves Klein, Lucio Fontana, Gordon Matta-Clark...), degradation (Klein again, Alberto Burri, Andy Warhol, Claes Oldenburg...), entropy (Jackson Pollock, Robert Smithson...), and to an exhausted disgusting materiality (Francis Bacon, Joseph Beuys, Damien Hirst...) whose "climax" was undoubtedly Piero Manzoni's *Artist's Shit*.

Paradoxically, this corrupted vision, more than plausible in a self-referential and descriptive sector like the world of art,[22] represents the operative horizon of some of the most interesting and innovative proposals recently advanced in architecture. Paradoxically because our discipline cannot limit itself to a representative, detached condition and must aim to negotiating with reality, responding to its needs. In other words, the "architect's shit" must smell of violets... In architecture perceptive inversion, dislocation of value and decontextualization can only act by identifying specific benefits. An example of this is the proposal advanced by Gilles Clément, agronomist and garden designer, for the identification of a "third landscape"[23] formed by those abandoned interstitial spaces whose indeterminate status has favoured a particular quality based on biodiversity. Although it resembles a landscaping project in the way it brings about a shift in focus capable of overturning the relationship between figure and background, in quantitative terms it has nothing in common with the nostalgia typical of the romantic tradition and its fascination with ruins. The latter is pataphysically overturned by the work in progress of the Alterazioni Video collective which explores the *Incompiuto siciliano*[24] (Unfinished buildings in Sicily), drawing up a manifesto celebrating the island's unusual capacity to produce public buildings that are left unfinished (due to the evident pre-eminence of other objectives), recognizing its distinctive "style" and promoting it the creation of "archaeological parks"...

If, as Marc Augé[25] suggests, history no longer has the time to produce ruins, just an increasing quantity of waste, the latter will end up by forming the context

and materials of contemporary architecture. Following in the wake of spontaneous phenomena like the recycling hippy communities of the 1960s,[26] even disciplinary contexts have begun to recognize this condition, first through the theoretical contributions of Martin Pawley[27] and Kevin Lynch,[28] then through Rural Studio's[29] structures made from car tyres and car windows (where residual construction materials echoed the social emargination of the clients), the 2012 Dutch projects intercepting flows of locally available materials and re-using them as part of their "normal" professional practice,[30] and then through the multiplication of occasions for the reconversion of polluted sites and dumps.[31]

All these proposals are intended to contain and secure waste, extracting positive values and reintroducing it into the flow in the form of recycled materials resembling virgin materials yet even more desirable due to their ability to silence our guilty feelings. One of the few practices dealing with waste as such, maintaining all its sulphurous potential exploited by the world of art, is the French R&Sie[(n)] group.[32] Their projects, cladding Bangkok's contemporary art museum in an electrostatic skin attracting particulates suspended in the city's polluted air, sucking the foul water of the Venetian lagoon between the transparent walls of a new university building, and capturing mosquitoes in the wall cavity of a house-trap in the Caribbean, all intensify the ill-ease, fear and disgust linked to a materiality so exhausted and disquieting as capable of producing a significant cast-off.

[1] MVRDV, *Metacity Datatown* (Rotterdam: 010 Publishers, 1999). | [2] *Wall-E*, directed by Andrew Stanton, Disney-Pixar, 2008. | [3] *Balle*, in Italian slang, means "lies." | [4] Don DeLillo, *Underworld* (New York: Scribner, 1997). | [5] David Foster Wallace, *Infinite Jest* (Boston, Massachusetts: Little, Brown, 1996). | [6] Francis Fukuyama, *The End of History and the Last Man* (New York: Free Press, 1992). | [7] Data from Chris Hails, ed., *Living Planet Report 2006* (Washington DC: WWF, 2006). | [8] William McDonough and Michael Braungart, *Cradle to Cradle: Remaking the Way We Make Things* (San Francisco: North Point Press, 2002). | [9] "An ecosystem might actually have more of a chance to become healthy and whole again after a quick collapse that leaves some niches intact than with a slow, deliberate and efficient destruction of the whole," ibid, p. 63. | [10] Renier de Graaf, interviewed by Christian Ernsten and Arjen Oosterman, "Up-tempo Urbanism," *Volume* 16 (2008). | [11] "The richest 10% of Canadian households create an ecological footprint of 12.4 hectares per capita—nearly two-and-a-half times that of the poorest 10%," http://www.hans.org/magazine/391/ecological-footprint-matters-canada. | [12] Matt Lewis, "Packaging Utopian Sustainability," *Volume* 16 (2008). | [13] Zygmunt Bauman, *Wasted Lives: Modernity and its Outcasts* (Cambridge, UK: Polity Press, 2004). | [14] John Roberts, interviewed by Piet Vollaard, "Yes, We Can... Up to a Point," *Volume* 18 (2008). | [15] Slavoj Žižek, "Censorship Today: Violence or Ecology as a New Opium for the Masses," *Volume* 18 (2008), p. 47. | [16] MVRDV, *KM3. Excursion on Capacities* (Barcelona: Actar, 2005). | [17] Rem Koolhaas, "Junkspace," *Oma@work, A+U* special issue (2000), p. 21. | [18] Ibid, p. 17. | [19] Ibid. | [20] *Das Unheimliche*, 1919. For an acute scrutiny of what is "disturbing" in contemporary architecture see Anthony Vidler, *The Architectural Uncanny: Essays in the Modern Unhomely* (Cambridge, Massachusetts: Mit Press, 1992). | [21] See Yve-Alain Bois and Rosalind Krauss, *Formless: A Users Guide* (New York: Zone Books, 1997). | [22] See Lea Vergine, *When Trash Becomes Art: Trash Rubbish Mongo* (Milan: Skira, 2007). | [23] Gilles Clément, *Manifeste du tiers paysage* (Paris: Sujet/Objet, 2004). | [24] Alterazioni Video, "Sicilian Incompletion," *Abitare* 486 (2008). | [25] Marc Augé, *Le temps en ruines* (Paris: Galilée, 2003). | [26] Alessandra Ponte, "Art and Garbage," *Lotus* 128 (2006). | [27] Martin Pawley, *Garbage Housing* (London: Architectural Press, 1975); Id., *Building for Tomorrow: Putting Waste to Work* (San Francisco: Sierra Club, 1982). | [28] Kevin Lynch, *Wasting Away. An Exploration of Waste: What It Is, How It Happens, Why We Fear It, How to Do It Well*, with contributions by Michael Southworth (San Francisco: Sierra Club, 1990). | [29] Andrea Oppenheimer Dean, *Rural Studio: Samuel Mockbee and an Architecture of Decency* (New York: Princeton Architectural Press, 2002). | [30] Ed van Hinte, Césare Peeren and Jan Jongert, *Superuse: Constructing New Architecture by Shortcutting Material Flows* (Rotterdam: 010 Publishers, 2007). 2012 Architecten and Suite75 also promote the online community superuse.org which allows users to post examples of design based on recycling. | [31] Julie Bargmann, *Toxic Beauty* (New York: Princeton Architectural Press, 2005); Peter Reed, *Groundswell: Constructing the Contemporary Landscape* (Basel: Birkhäuser, 2005); Deborah Gans and Claire Weisz, eds., *Extreme Sites: The "Greening" of Brownfield, Architectural Design* 168 (2004) | [32] Giovanni Corbellini, *Bioreboot: The Architecture of R&Sie(n)* (New York: 22 Publishing and Princeton Architectural Press, 2009).

Enrico Fontanari

Urban
Arrange

ments

Today's interest in abandoned zones or zones using abandoned objects, in discarded territories and landscapes, along with the international debate on the landscape of waste project have all moved the focus of urban and regional projects from mitigation-renewal-regeneration to recycling the products of transformations caused by development.[1]

In the architectural and urban planning sector, recycling is now seen as a strategic choice offering outstanding opportunities to create new uses, new meanings, new forms of modernness and a renewed capacity to respond to the contemporary demand for dwelling quality. The hypothesis explored in this paper is that in order to construct new meanings through recycling you need to propose new arrangements of discarded materials, including waste generated by contemporary urban and regional growth and transformation processes.

We must try to "arrange" objects, thoughts, concepts without aiming to order or explain, but seeking to illustrate a reflection, to develop a line of reasoning or observation, using an unexpected, novel arrangement unlike the previous one to draw attention to a problem or question.

Re-order, re-arrange, re-signify. The aim of this group of actions is to avoid merely freezing the status quo and overcome that tendency, still strongly present today, to use memory as a nostalgic and paralyzing regret. "Dead" objects whose purpose and use are at an end can come back to life through new arrangements, new juxtapositions that give them new meanings and functions.

How can we arrange something without this action producing "waste"? Maybe it is impossible, maybe waste is inevitable, unless we consider a situation in constant movement, an uninterrupted process of change transforming what has been created. That is, if we assume that our arrangement is provisional. Accepting the concept of "provisional" means dropping the idea of arranging things according to a rule that is clear-cut and unchanging. The challenge is to try and organize a kind of "reign of chaos," arranging our objects/concepts in that grey area separating "useful products" from waste, in the kingdom of the indefinite, of the uncertain, of danger.

OPPOSITES AND JUXTAPOSITIONS: THE ARTISTIC ACTION

Precariousness and stability, provisional arrangement and permanence, or rather, duration. An oxymoron. A beautiful arrangement tends towards perfection and should last for ever. But what happens if a new beautiful arrangement shows up? How can we reconcile beauty and precariousness?

Many contemporary artists are going in this direction. Just consider the revealing action involved in Christo and Jeanne-Claude's "wrapping" of monuments or well as Peter Greenaway's recent reinterpretations of celebrated artworks of the past.[2] Under Greenaway's guidance, the audience moves and re-arranges the objects/subjects of the painting according to a new point of view put forward by the director. And rearranging them it carries out a "resignification" of the artwork concerned.

Another powerful example of resignification through re-arrangement—in this case of the waste of everyday family life—was carried out by the Chinese artist Song Dong in his *Waste Not* installation, which has travelled to various countries since its debut in 2005.[3] "The installation is nothing but a random collection of discarded objects,"[4] hoarded over the decades by the artist's mother, Zhao Xiangyuan (from the 1950s to 2005), with the aim of not wasting anything and exploiting the possibility of reusing used objects and the discards of domestic activities or housework.[5] By tidying away in an "orderly manner" all the objects that she and her family used in their everyday life, Xiangyuan succeeds in revealing that grey area separating what is "useful" from "waste." The order is only defined by the way objects with similar uses and original functions (saucepans, blankets, plastic tops, toothpaste tubes, shoes, clothes, etc.) are placed side by side or stacked up, tidied away and rearranged so that they take up less space and are easier to find, identify, and, where possible, recycle.

Zhao Xiangyuan's artist son, Song Dong, who will transform this extraordinary habit into an internationally successful installation and exhibition, realizes that his mother's decision not to get rid of or throw away objects that have reached the end of their useful lives, and instead hoarding, ordering and rearranging them, endows them with a new value. Ordering the waste makes it evident and gives it dignity. In other words, it shifts the boundaries between "accepted" and "discarded." By transforming this activity into an account, into a story,[6] Song Dong bestows upon waste the "historic" dignity traditionally reserved for products. He shows how waste or objects discarded after being used up/worn out can become part of the creative process once their "official" useful life is over.

The importance of juxtaposition relative to arrangement also emerges from conditions laid down by the contemporary art collector, G. Panza di Biumo, when disposing of groups of works from his vast collection. He established that works by the same artist were to be kept together, either in a single room or space, in order to focus on the process of research carried out by the artist rather than on the mere aesthetic valence of the object produced.

New arrangements and juxtapositions can be used to reveal differences and prevent the predominance of an idea/image of uniformity resulting from superficial observation and favoured by repetition of similar situations. It was this type of thought that caused the curators of the Tate Modern to eschew chronological order or schools in favour of thematic groups when deciding how to display the gallery's permanent collection of contemporary art. The unexpected "juxtaposition" forces viewers to participate more attentively, inspiring deeper reflection.

But the possibility of carrying out new arrangements is not necessarily limited to temporary installation. Objects can be arranged differently for long periods of time, the important thing is to always allow for change and accommodate the temporary aspect. And not to seek perfection, which opposes change. The arrangement as we see it here implies change, modification.

These are different ways of using the arrangement of objects to draw attention to themes, problems or reflections that would otherwise escape us. These are ways of continuously giving new life, new functions and, above all, new meaning to objects that would otherwise be condemned to just one type of use and to being discarded—the condition preceding their entry to the inexorable world of waste—once that use was over or "consumed."

LANDSCAPE AND URBANISM

In the midst of today's discussions on the crisis of the city and, above all, of town planning, we must recognize the failure of the twentieth-century reformist dream to which this discipline owes so much, the end of the dream that we could induce or govern modifications.

That sense of limit that characterized the feeling of belonging to a city right from its very beginnings to the twentieth century has vanished. The contemporary city has no limits. It has "exploded."[7] Although the city originally implied a concept of boundary, today that city-form has broken, and city and hinterland are physically superimposed, they share the same dimensions. Contemporary cities can no longer be distinguished from their hinterland. They have lost their finite character.

As a result, town planning based on separating functions (the zoning of the Modern Movement) has been superseded. Now everything mingles and integrates.

We are witnessing a major loss of references. The failure of the Modern Movement's idea of city, widely recognized during the latter half of the "short century"[8] and now accompanied by the virtual impossibility of conceiving and, therefore, of planning new models of cities, has caused us to revise our attitudes to the modern, forcing us to rethink the very concept of modern. That idea of city was rooted in a shared vision of the urban dimension whereby the city was something coherent and circumscribed whose boundaries could be overcome but only in order to be redefined, redesigned. Now we must recognize that "urbanism [...] has disappeared at the moment when urbanization everywhere [...] is on its way to establishing a definitive, global 'triumph' of the urban condition," that the processes and dimensions of contemporary construction of cities throughout the world have turned "the professionals of the city [into] chess players who lose to computers."[9]

Today's overriding uncertainty causes us to tackle matters in fragments. The dominant vision of the city is now "fractal," the prevailing approach is one of "dismantlement": "The world is decomposed into incompatible fractals of uniqueness, each a pretext for further disintegration of the whole: a paroxysm of fragmentation that turns the particular into a system."[10]

Can we attempt to design new fragments and reorganize urban spaces without constructing new cities, defining new models, "resolving" urban problems or re-forming the city? Maybe landscaping tradition, or rather landscapers' approach to design can once more come to our aid. By that I mean the approach emerging from recent debate and not those impossible projects for large open spaces popular during the eighteenth and nineteenth centuries, and right up to the avant-garde period. Landscaping, a discipline originally spanning the areas of reform (especially urban reform) and design, has also experienced interesting developments in recent years.

One consequence of the end of the reformist dream, of "reform" as an instrument for the creation of new broad and stable forms of organization for society and its spatial layout, was the emergence of uncertainty and unstability as dominant characteristics in social relations and therefore in spatial organization. Another was a growing attention to the processual and relational aspects of society, and therefore movement, fluidity in uses of space, that forced the interpretation of urban space to recognize new categories: from the compact city to dispersion, to the network city and to the generic city.

Thus, uncertainty and fragmentariness accompany our recognition of the dominance of these processual and relational natures, our attention to

the concepts of mobility and fluidity. Thanks to these new approaches we can imagine grafting the contribution of landscaping tradition onto town planning, an "urban planning saved by landscaping."[11] We could retrieve the traditional approach of landscaping projects, their attention to the processual nature of transformations, their different approach to the duration of a project and their acceptance of their provisional nature, their non-finiteness and their progressive transformability, the way their project proposal incorporates the concept of "progressive modification."

POINTS OF VIEW, LANDSCAPE AND CONTEMPORARY CITY

If we consider the fact that the concept of landscape is the outcome of a subjective action, we could imagine using the landscape as a way of observing the local context.

The landscaping vision can play a role in local planning, in the construction of a local planning project: urban dispersion and fragmentation of landscapes are complementary. Landscape and its changes now affect us more strongly, and immersing ourselves in today's landscape can help us understand the problems and contradictions of contemporary living as well as helping us understand new values. Looking at, observing landscape and its evolution can help us understand its changes. Our observation of abandoned places and wasted areas forces us to learn from the changes that have taken place in the spatial organization of the city's hinterland, laying the foundations for the process intelligence now indispensable for our ability to understand and intervene in local transformation processes. One of the profound implications of the reference to landscape is a rejection of fixed forms in favour of processuality and the possibility of setting into motion virtuous processes by re-placing, re-arranging objects and situations.

But applied to the city this implies agreeing not to prefigure new physical spaces and social relations that are somehow definite, pre-ordered, and to work in terms of fragments, actions-in-progress, with the aim of setting into motion processes of transformation or new forms of land use that are not completely defined and where the final result has not been laid down. Our project for the future is not an object, a product or design, but a process, a path whose instability and uncertainty is no mystery to us.

One of the possible aims of the project for the transformation of the status quo could involve shifting the boundaries between useful and waste in cities and their hinterlands. Instead of restoring or regenerating we could try revealing the "beauty" of waste and focusing on the possibility of "arranging" parts of the city that are now separated or detached in new ways/forms. Acting upon the city, both formal and informal, as Greenaway did with Veronese, revealing and collecting contents and narratives unlike the ones that can be observed with a superficial glance. And so doing, re-signifying the single parts.

There are several examples of recent town-planning projects where a new approach, the observation of urban reality from a different point of view, have played a key role in revealing the potential importance and centrality of an urbanscape traditionally held to be peripheral and chaotic.

Although an ordered space is a space governed by rules, rules are such by virtue of their ability to prohibit and exclude, and therefore potentially produce waste. One of the most extensive forms of waste produced by town-planning is the informal city, a concept characterizing most of the world's contemporary urban spaces that is no longer a marginal phenomenon but a new structural reality. Thanks to a new point of view (a capacity to establish relationships rather than collect images), the informal city has been transformed from waste into a new form, a new component of the city, that has given rise to numerous real improvements in the dwelling conditions and general standards of living of its inhabitants.

This is what happens when you take the main urban roads, cycle paths and public transport to the informal city to make it accessible,[12] libraries and aerial tramways to the suburbs,[13] parks into inhabited cemeteries,[14] and arrange urban facilities and infrastructure differently, thus attempting to re-arrange parts of the city and contrasting social universes. The final aim of such actions is not so much inclusion (who includes whom?) as hybridization that ensues from the juxtaposition of different urban and social realities.

LANDSCAPE OF WASTE: RESISTANCE/RESILIENCE

The shift in focus from regeneration to recycling implies that projects have adopted the concept of "transformation" as a tenet. But when we take action to transform an existing object, while maintaining it, we also assume the concept of a modification of its nature, of its value: use, aesthetic, symbolic and memory value.

In the project process recovery/regeneration and recycling are distinguished by various conceptual differences. One of these concerns the idea of

conserving, which is often linked to a need to order, to re-order. Recycling, on the other hand, leads to a new arrangement of objects and re-arrangement. Not just modification of objects, therefore, but above all construction of a new order, regardless of how knowingly provisional.

When we deal with the theme of recycling we need to be prepared to establish the criteria that we will use to modify the "arrangement" of the objects involved. Then we re-order them and so doing find ourselves having to tackle the problem of defining a limit, a boundary (a transient one) within whose confines we must re-order our objects.

We need to look at waste objects not in terms of what they are but in terms of what they could potentially become. Somehow the landscape of waste manages to stimulate our project visions. If we agree that understanding means creating then we have to recognize that the architectural, local or landscaping project must create the necessary dynamics to help us comprehend something that could not otherwise be entirely understood.

On the one hand, we can see that the contemporary city grows out of the constant addition of roads, houses, containers, sheds, that it is the outcome of a series of single actions that have created the current morphology of the built world step by step. It is a hybrid city, the result of a summation of individual stories.

On the other, we know that landscape is the image of a geography created by the culture that built it and that the values of a community are revealed by its shaping. While easy to understand in the case of rural landscape, how is a community's culture reflected in an urban landscape? And in the landscape of waste? Rearranging the objects of the landscape of waste provides us with an occasion for building new cultural awareness for the communities that generated that waste.

The true challenge facing projects in contemporary urban reality is not so much the question of identity but the theme of the recognizability of territories and landscapes, and therefore of places. Recognizability may extend to processes, facilitating process intelligence, helping us to grasp the potential of ongoing processes as well as foreseeing the limits of development.

By looking at waste differently, we can also free ourselves from having to assume a "resistential" attitude to the impact of development and at the same time not limit ourselves to merely seeking resilient project responses to the ongoing transformation processes.

If we are aware of our subjectiveness when we observe the territory through the landscaping filter, then we must consider our observation of the landscape of waste as an opportunity for overcoming the resistance/resilience alternative, as a situation that is in some respects extreme and that forces us to think, create new objects, new realities and relations, unexpected landscapes. We need to rediscover various approaches arising out of the concept of sub-urbanism, like, for example, the site invents the programme and the site is the matrix of the programme.[15] The various sites should be grouped in complete freedom, developing the ability to grasp what time—and not tradition—has brought to the planners' drawing boards. We should think of city projects as the outcome of a journey, a process, as a search for innovation and not a preordained design. As something that does not necessarily produce cities in the twentieth-century sense of the term alluded before.

Today's focus on the new arrangement of waste can lead us to develop project tactics rather than strategies, using concepts like recycling, juxtaposing, and hybridizing. It can inspire us to work without presumptions on commercial spaces, on new public spaces and on the waste of urban sprawl,[16] on the mobility networks and their potential. In urban environments, not only do infrastructures and the organization of mobility and accessibility in general allow us to see different landscapes, sometimes in the space of a single day, they also allow us to juxtapose them, while commuting.

From this point of view, the landscape of waste can help us construct a tactical approach, to enter the flow of processes, to grasp and oversee things, without straining spontaneity but at the same time recognizing the tactical role of the resilient approach rather than considering it a strategic choice. Aware of the limits of a purely tactical vision. Yet another consequence of focusing on the landscape of waste is to reveal the demand for a strategic vision—currently pending—and the need to adopt a strategic approach even during the construction of strongly fragmented and temporally fluid spatial realities.

[1] Although the bibliography on this topic is extensive, major works include the following: James Corner, ed., *Recovering Landscape* (New York: Princeton Architectural Press, 1999); Alan Berger, *Drosscape. Wasting Land in Urban America* (New York, Princeton Architectural Press, 2006); Charles Waldheim, ed., *The Landscape Urbanism Reader* (New York: Princeton Architectural Press, 2006); Sara Marini, *Architettura parassita. Strategie di riciclaggio per la città* (Macerata: Quodlibet, 2008); the texts and bibliography assembled on the occasion of the conference organized by ECLAS on "Landscapes & Ruins. Planning and Design for Derelict Places," Genoa, 23–26 September 2009.

[2] These projects propose new readings and interpretations of famous works like Rembrandt's *Nightwatch* and Leonardo's *Last Supper*. They include the installation set up in the Palladian refectory on the Island of San Giorgio in 2009 reinterpreting Veronese's *Wedding at Cana*.

[3] "*Waste Not* is an enormous art installation made of over ten thousand of worn, broken, and occasionally unused objects, the majority of which would be considered garbage in any other situation," from Wu Hung, *Waste Not: Zhao Xiangyuan & Song Dong* (Tokyo: Tokyo Gallery + BTAP, 2009).

[4] Ibid.

[5] The country experienced a period of great economic difficulty from the late 1950s to the end of the 1960s with many people living in conditions of extreme poverty, worsened in the case of those like Xiangyuan who were relatives of people condemned for political motives.

[6] What makes this installation so interesting is not so much its use of ready-made objects, which is traditional in contemporary art, but their arrangement not just by type but according to associations and juxtapositions

responding to practical, emotional and moral considerations.

7 Francesco Indovina, Laura Fregolent, Michelangelo Savino, eds., *L'esplosione della città* (Bologna: Compositori, 2005).

8 This theme has been dealt with by a vast body of works, both numerous and very different—from Rem Koolhaas' 1978 *Delirious New York* to Bernard Huet's article "The City as Dwelling Space: Alternatives to the Charter of Athens," in *Lotus International* 41 (1984), etc.—that I will refrain from listing in full because it would be impossible to reflect the scope and variety of positions characterizing this debate at the end of the twentieth century.

9 Rem Koolhaas and Bruce Mau, *S, M, L, XL* (1995) (New York: The Monacelli Press, 1998).

10 Ibid.

11 Paraphrasing the title of a *lectio magistralis* by Bernardo Secchi, "L'architettura salvata dall'urbanistica" (Architecture saved by urban planning), given in Venice, at the IUAV University, at the opening ceremony of the 1993–94 academic year.

12 Projects implemented in Curitiba (Brazil) and Bogotá (Colombia).

13 Schemes carried out in Caracas (Venezuela) and Medellin (Colombia).

14 Project promoted by the Aga Khan Centre in the city of Cairo (Egypt).

15 Sébastien Marot, *Sub-urbanisme and the Art of Memory* (London: AA Publications, 2003).

16 From abandoned industrial hangars to the numerous fringe areas produced by infrastructure or other projects, the cross-section of wasted land in urbanized regions is extremely vast. These abandoned areas represent opportunities for various types of project, like, for example, settling collective service activities and favouring new settlements in order to reach the minimum threshold required to supply services.

Alberto Bertagna

Digestio
Separate
Collectio

s.
Project
n

Digestion is a chemical and mechanical transformation process that acts upon a given substance, attacking it, breaking it down and converting it into something else. A project is a physical and cultural process that modifies a context. It measures itself against the status and dynamics of the context, breaks it down into simple elements and relations and then projects a recomposed version of it in a different way. Digestion is a form of catabolism or simplification; it reduces complex molecules into simpler ones. The project negotiates the articulation of a context, inevitably bringing about a partition of what is real. Digestion is a selection process. It decides how much of the given substance is necessary, rejects the waste (at least where possible) but produces it. Whether by choice or not, projects also deal with what is (no longer) accepted, developing its story, introducing other directions and eliminating other scenarios. It produces waste even when dealing with or using it. Digestion is a primary process; without its intervention nothing is possible. Similarly, the antecedence of a projection with regard to action is a primary condition of society even before architecture. Once it has been set off, digestion is irreversible. It is only interrupted in isolated cases and its failure to proceed usually compromises the system to which it belongs. A project sets off causal chains even when it tries to make them casual. Digestion, though largely involuntary, is a dependent process; infinite interacting variables complicate its simplicity and linearity although not, at least when it works, the outcome. A project, in its becoming, depends on the "noise" that may from time to time adjust the imagined direction, a noise that may often contribute to a birth.[1] Digestion somehow takes place via secret channels. We see what we injest and, although it may be "base materialism" or "scatology,"[2] to say it with Georges Bataille and Bois-Krauss, we also see what we expel. What we save remains a mystery, even though the outcomes of this act of salvation are evident; they basically consist of ourselves, of what we see in the mirror. Our project, our "becoming-other" can but come about through digestion. We are what we eat, or rather, to paraphrase Ludwig Feuerbach,[3] we will be what we have digested.

Digestion, in short, is a project of appropriation. It evolves our being through what is other than us. Thanks to it we introject the external world for our own ends, our use and consumption.

• • •

Before developing our line of reasoning, we need to include additional premises in order to understand *what* we are introjecting from that world into the project "for our use and consumption," what we are appropriating, and finally, what consumption itself, and therefore waste, could mean in the context of this essay and how we intend to *deal with them*. If we are to reflect on our eating habits and on what feeds us, and equally to understand how a context can be turned into a programme and then into a landscape, given that this question lies at the heart of our past behaviour and overlaps into the area of anthropology, we can but turn to Claude Lévi-Strauss' "Culinary Triangle." Nothing useful on the geometric front. Despite the significance of this figure for us, we will not dwell on problems of form as much as the space between those vertices: this is where our *Landscape of Waste* lies, between Raw, Cooked and Rotten. This is, after all, where we started out. With the chemical and mechanical and physical and cultural processes of transformation. With digestion. And maybe before proceeding (swallowing?), we should take note of the other words indirectly linked to our preamble, words that will directly or indirectly feed this entire process, without envisaging any form of defecation—to remain with the "scatological" theme mentioned above—thus possibly suspending it without concluding it, without outlining too many "relations" with what was introduced. Because in addition to *alteration* we have already discussed *reduction*, *choice*, *antecedence*, *dependence*, *irreversibility*, *secrecy* and *appropriation*. And dwelling upon or merely touching upon these terms we will seek to reach what we intend to assert: that the project must be a kind of separate waste collection, highlighting differences rather than their solution, glue or amalgam;[4] that the project must lack relations in order to allow them to truly exist; that only if it is imagined enclosed in subsequent processes (though independent, non-relational even in time), processes anticipating examination, separation or self-sacrifice, can it truly pro-pose itself or others; that it may pre-scind from the need for its own usefulness; that only its pre-visional action is preventive.

And so, to return to Lévi-Strauss, to his semantic field outlined using three points, and to our first word, we should immediately point out that everything taking place in the creation of the *Landscape of Waste* can be described by referring to the segments linking cooked, raw and putrid: cultural transformation and natural transformation are what precede and make true our digestion, our project-making: everything by means of which we make the real be other than itself and everything by means of which we become; everything that we appropriate, and which we could or should do without.

Nor should we consider this "we make" an immodest statement: even where raw naturally proceeds to putrid, even where the project does not block the decay but lets it develop, it nevertheless intervenes, albeit not in a direct manner. Though it may stand on the sidelines, even the most indifferent project relates to it. Let us leave subtle Straussian specifications here; no "refinement" of our discourse. We are not saying that for varying cultures putrid could also be a product of human interpolation (French cheese for the Allied soldiers after the Normandy landings). We are not relativizing matters: even in the natural transition—non-human, absolutely spontaneous and unprovoked transition—from raw to putrid, the project acts: maybe because it can smell its stench and moves away from it. Nor do we want to go too far into the French anthropologist's theories: boiled, roast or smoked food, the sense of what we are trying to affirm would be lost among recipes and customs. Our sole interest is in identifying the extent to which something may lie between cooked and raw, raw and putrid, putrid and cooked, something arising from those chemical and physical and cultural and mechanical processes that could be of interest to us: an *alteration* in other words. It is not the *taste* variation ensuing from such transitions that concerns us here, but the *physical* variation. If we refer back to the guiding words introduced

above, we will see that *antecedence* is not only involved in the process from digestion to action or pro-ject to object, but also from cooking to nutrition. In the same way, before cooking an *appropriation* must take place. Leaving aside the obvious *choice* that is made with regard to an offer that is total for us omnivores (widespread availability to which the diffusion of our species at local level, our appropriation of every context, is linked); the *reduction* involved in every cooking procedure or process of decomposition; or the *secrecy* of certain recipes (the role of "mystery" as a vector of social hierarchization is well-known, the mechanism of stewardship and limited transmission of knowledge in order to maintain Power over the Other, incapable alone to interpret and assume the positive aspects of the world, this process that makes "reserved" a commodity of control and authority—of project, projection towards the Other—could be better explained by Lévi-Strauss himself); without entering into the merits of cooking "procedures," into its *dependences*, its *irreversability*. Without necessarily exploring all these aspects, maybe just placing them, and their implications, alongside the first one, let's just dwell on that word *alteration* for a moment.

• • •

"One morning, as I was passing through the Grand Canal in Venice on a vaporetto, someone suddenly pointed out to me Filarete's column and the Vicolo del Duca and the humble houses constructed where the ambitious palace of this Milanese lord was to have been. I always observe this column and its base, this column that is both a beginning and an end. This document or relict of time, in its absolute formal purity, has always seemed to me a symbol of architecture consumed by the life which surrounds it. I have rediscovered Filarete's column in the Roman ruins at Budapest, in the transformation of certain amphitheaters, and above all as one possible fragment of a thousand other buildings."[5]

• • •

Everything of interest to us here—our *Landscape of Waste*—lives in and around this term,

MONDIAL ATOMIC ENERGY PRODUCTION

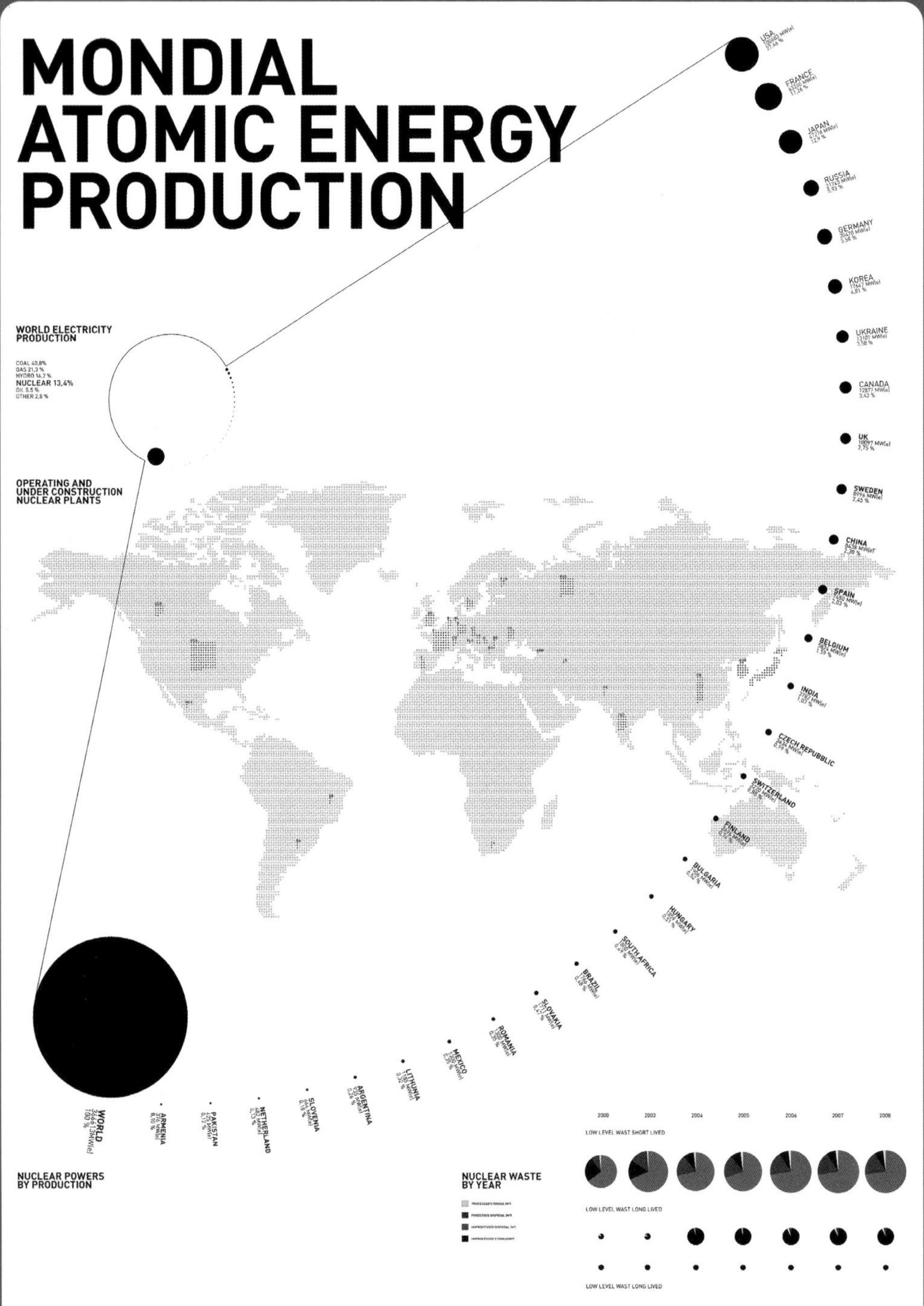

WORLD ELECTRICITY PRODUCTION

COAL 40,8%
GAS 21,3 %
HYDRO 16,7 %
NUCLEAR 13,4%
OIL 5,5 %
OTHER 2,5 %

OPERATING AND UNDER CONSTRUCTION NUCLEAR PLANTS

USA
(101 MWe)
31,06 %

FRANCE
11,34 %

JAPAN
11,9 %

RUSSIA
5,93 %

GERMANY
5,58 %

KOREA
4,81 %

UKRAINE
3,58 %

CANADA
3,43 %

UK
2,70 %

SWEDEN
2,45 %

CHINA

SPAIN
2,03 %

BELGIUM

INDIA
1,32 %

CZECH REPUBLIC

SWITZERLAND

FINLAND

BULGARIA

HUNGARY

SOUTH AFRICA

BRAZIL

ROMANIA

SLOVAKIA

MEXICO

LITHUANIA

ARGENTINA

SLOVENIA

NETHERLAND

PAKISTAN

ARMENIA

WORLD

NUCLEAR POWERS BY PRODUCTION

NUCLEAR WASTE BY YEAR

PRODUCED SHORT LIVED
PROCESSED SHORT LIVED
UNPROCESSED SHORT LIVED
UNPROCESSED LONG LIVED

| 2000 | 2003 | 2004 | 2005 | 2006 | 2007 | 2008 |

LOW LEVEL WAST SHORT LIVED

LOW LEVEL WAST LONG LIVED

LOW LEVEL WAST LONG LIVED

106

42

6 August 1945, Hiroshima (Japan)

50

TIME
ERRORS
FATE

22 July 1958, Bikini (Isole Marshall)

alteration. And it is here that we act to keep what we need edible, otherwise deciding to forgo or exclude. To avoid alteration or to resolve, to eliminate it. But alteration is not a direct process. It goes through intermediate levels. It is progressive and may be what happens to a programme, a prevision, a project. An alteration may also be a pause. An "ambitious palace" becomes, becoming democratic, throwing off the garb of "project" (in the "authorial" sense of the expression), becoming improvised and plural, "humble houses"; "Filarete's column" ("a possible fragment") sees only its context changed: it basically remains the same, lacking spasms "in its absolute formal purity." We will then take a look at what this "withdrawal" of the project could mean, what its making room for spontaneity could mean. Let's focus on this line of possibility, on the force of the column in itself. Let's try to reach one of the theories we alluded to above: the need to leave behind the relational aspect in landscape planning. To go back just one step, what aspects of the cooked-raw-putrid triangle are of interest to us? The transition between the steps. What changes in this natural-artificial evolution? Only the *duration* of the commodities. In the Straussian triangle, if the "natural" process links directly to the raw, the top vertex, to the putrid, bottom right-hand vertex, then the "cooked," bottom left-hand vertex, is merely a step, a slowing down of the anti-clockwise movement going from raw to putrid: cooking is a device that is capable of increasing the number of photograms in the time unit, delaying the projected action or moving the direct evolution backwards in time (and here Lévi-Strauss codified positions and directions according to his own cultural background: its natural evolution as a historical process, a time-schedule in fact; the artificial transformation as anti-historic, the shift back in time—cooking increases the duration, cooking that almost involves an anterior transition, antecedent to the raw in the inexorable progress towards the putrid—like an anti-clockwise movement). But duration here does not have an absolute value. It is not a quality in itself: duration is obviously linked to a meaning, it is a "period of useful time." What changes after all is what transforms, it is the

usefulness of the product. If time is the regulatory principle, then the organizing principle is exploitation: artificial, cultural actions are governed by the wish to increase, to extend the acquisition of a benefit.

So let's try to reach a preliminary, partial conclusion in order to proceed in our reasoning: those tensions, those relations linking the terms, linking *objects* through *actors* in time, are actually models for using the world, the context. On the one hand (from raw to cooked to putrid), exploitation proceeds towards maximization: the time of our capacity to appropriate the Other expands, space increases, the stretch that can be travelled along extends. On the opposite side, the time-schedule side (from raw to putrid) must necessarily augment the intensity of our hold on the world, the risk otherwise is that our energy decreases.

But what would happen if the organizing principle of the lines of power (power of appropriation) was no longer exploitation? What would be triggered if we stopped considering putrid, raw and cooked in terms of their different degrees of usefulness? What would we obtain if we managed to suspend our judgement from an assessment of productivity, satisfaction and therefore of *taste*?

• • •

"More than that, as a dead man on reprieve, the dying man *falls* outside the *thinkable*, which is identified with what one can *do*. In leaving the field circumscribed by the possibilities of treatment, it enters a region of meaninglessness. Nothing can be said in a place where nothing more can be done. Along with the lazy man, and more than he, the dying man is the immoral man: the former, a subject that does not work; the latter, an object that no longer even makes itself available to be worked on by others; both are intolerable in a society in which the disappearance of subjects is everywhere compensated for and camouflaged by the multiplication of the tasks to be performed [...]. In our society, the absence of work is non-sense; it is necessary to eliminate it in order for the discourse that tirelessly articulates tasks and constructs the Occidental story of 'There's always something to do' to continue. The dying man is the lapse of this discourse. He is, and can only be, ob-scene. And hence censured, deprived of language, wrapped up in a shroud of silence: the unnamable."[6]

• • •

What would happen, what *Landscape of Waste* would we obtain if we stopped thinking of that column, of that "relict of time" exclusively, as an alternative to its defecation, as a "possible fragment of a thousand other buildings"? A fragment that is only useful in a perspective of re-use, reinsertion into a context; useful only if we envisage "tasks" for it, whatever they might be, inscribed within a relational setting; edible, assimilable by someone, together with something (lazy man requiring convincing), or otherwise "obscene," a dying man who is definitively expelled because impossible to reallocate among the "active ones." Here we must distinguish between the meaning of the column in Aldo Rossi's interpretation and the reality in which events progress. For the Milanese architect, that column was an example or synthesis of a projectual concept, of a way of developing projects. In history it appears as a merely casual event; it is a chance re-discovery, fortuitous waste, a free legacy. Still fit (for work), in both cases they are a "component" that is absorbed in a new discourse. While on the one hand it is still a potential project driver, though unaware of what it might become, on the other, that of the "humble houses," it is a negligible part. Its presence triggers relationality, though paratactic, on the one hand, indifference on the other.
In the perspective of the project that column is meaningful. A space and a time are *imagined* for it because it is assigned an essential task within a whole, firstly by the "Milanese gentlemen" then by Aldo Rossi. Once this "reason" is removed, it has no dignity to be saved. In everyday life however all that is *left* is a field of existence.
In the first case, it would have been necessary to for-see a new use for that column, a use that would have to dialogue with other voices in the long term because on its own its lacks purpose and is therefore mute.
In the second, time is compressed into the short, instant space of mere acceptance.

(And today, incidentally, that pre-vision must become even swifter in assigning roles, because— we could say—since the decline in the use of stone, the obsolescence of the world off which projects can feed has become almost instantaneous: that line between cooked and putrid—between object, body, their eliminability—shrinks.)
It is in the register of thought of usefulness that waste exists, in the dual role of *problem*, like the dying man, and *opportunity*, like the lazy man. It is in the register of thought of determinism that usefulness becomes "necessity," linked necessarily to a reason, a purpose, and therefore to a relation. Only by reasoning in the context of these consequentialities does the landscape of waste appear as a theme that must inevitably "be resolved," irresistibly caused to evolve towards a new horizon of meaning, whether one of gastric absorption, involvement as a part of/in a whole, or one of scatological defecation, exclusion as alien, and not as pure landscape "valid" in itself. Not only, today more than yesterday, "worthy" for the emergence of a changed sensibility, for the now accepted aesthetic of the "uncanny,"[7] so that these are "taste" evaluations that we said we wished to leave behind. Here we wish to welcome the dying man and the lazy man, leaving them as they are. The point is, or at least it seems to us, that consequentiality itself may no longer be a pursuable concept. That is why "Our" *Landscape of Waste* wishes to attempt to explore different scenarios, within which there may *possibly* be a reuse; just incidentally though, not intentionally. And the first vector of provenance and succession is the concept of relation: as we mentioned above, what we wish to reflect on is the relation between a body and a reason and a purpose. Let's restate it: the theory here is that we must leave behind the relational approach—with all the *physical* consequences that entails—and the demands of a project. Separation, separate waste collection must necessarily distinguish elements, not necessarily forcing them all towards an expectation, or involving them in a coherent or finalistic design, a teleological design, in a *normal* digestive process.

• • •

3 January 1961, Idaho Falls (USA)

28 March 1979, Three Mile Island (USA)

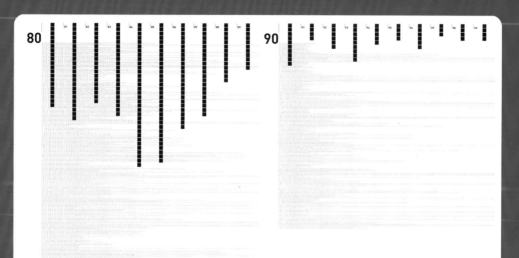

26 April 1986, Chernobyl (Ukraine)

"I had no pain—my hunger had taken the edge off it. In its stead I felt pleasantly empty, untouched by everything around me, and glad not to be noticed by any one. I put my feet up on the seat and leant back. Thus I could best appreciate the well-being of perfect isolation."[8]

• • •

Statutorily, the only way of understanding (intending and containing) the landscape is interpreting it in relational rather than objective terms. Right from the first conceptualizations, from its "literary" origins, from Petrarch's "Ventoux" onwards, we could say that "landscape" is the peak that has been *touched*: with our look, with our minds, or, with fatigue, following the paths leading up to it. The natural operational translation of that reading in the physical field—the disciplinary field of the project, of architecture, a city or a local area—comes into action when a component is added to the landscape encountered, detected, when a transformation is brought about, relating the new entity introduced, its spatiality or its signification, not just with the surrounding context in its present (with all the realities encountered, therefore also with the communities, with their needs and cultures), but also with its past and future. Thus the project becomes a process, of integration with what comes before and adjustment (*alteration*, to use our guiding word again) with respect to what is likely to come afterwards. It seems perfectly logical to imagine continuing with these assumptions also at a time when there is a tendency to consider every reality in terms of a landscape, ordinary as well as extraordinary ones, and therefore to deal with all landscapes, even landscapes of waste, applying also to them the hypothesis of a process-project capable of relating to everything found in the context (whatever entity, biological or otherwise, as well as memory), but also with its and its own evolution. Today it seems, however, that the project-process is not only forced to tackle an afterwards that prepares or anticipates, but an afterwards that could appear alien to what is expected; imagining itself faced with transience more than slow variations, both of the contexts and of its own previsions; imagining itself faced with fractures in time. Today it increasingly seems that the process should no longer be seen as a system of reception or partial exclusion, of choice, but as an exclusive system of leave-taking: a digestive process fundamentally designed for disposal, for the refusal of what it was about to do.

Faced with this changed conception, the different substance of becoming in contemporaneity (from the constantly "expiring" present of the existential reflections of Emil Cioran to the present increasingly crushed on the *current*, first of Edmund Husserl then of Gilles Deleuze, to the "blocked" present and "missed surprise" of Marc Augé); faced therefore with the subtraction of the future dimension, relationality with tomorrow, with what is likely to *occur*, it seems to be experiencing a crisis. But the condition of a contemporaneity lacking effective projective capacity is not the only factor causing a crisis in the pro-ject, shaking it right down to its etymological foundations, in its "relational" existence, deterministic in as far as it is linked to a purpose, to an objective to be reached. A second variable intervenes in compromising it in its role as operator capable of controlling the becoming. From James Maxwell's discontinuity to René Thom's "catastrophe," from Niels Bohr's principle of complementarity to Werner Heisenberg's indetermination, from studies on organizational systems and fortuitousness as an element of self-organization developed by Henri Atlan, to the epistemological observations of Emanuele Severino on relations between regulatory elements and systemic anomalies, complexity and non-linearity have definitively brought the principle of randomness to the brink of a crisis. Chance is no longer admitted but must become a founding element for every reflection on becoming. The principle whereby conditions established correspond to predictable outcomes has been stripped of every certainty.

• • •

"Our capacity for "doing" is now far greater than our capacity to "foreseeing" the effects of our doing."[9]

• • •

In Knut Hamsun's hallucinated world,
where gastric processes are wiped out by the
cancellation of nutrition, where the protagonist's
Hunger defines his entire journey, where his *search*
for hunger, his deliberate *refusal* of nutrition
is a metaphor for his rejection of society, of social
relations, of encountering the other, of relationality,
interpreted as a factor of moral compromise
of one's self (a *desire for hunger as strength*);[10] right
there, between the depression and euphoria
of the protagonist, between appetite and nausea,
something takes place that could be extremely
interesting to us, for the purposes of our
reasoning.[11] In that Christiania landscape becomes
exclusively non-relational, time freezes in a repetitive
vacuum, suspended in absence of new events
and projects: and the final rent, his escape from
that world, takes place with no forewarning.[12]
The protagonist does not appropriate "anything,"
his hunger is his isolation from the world: he only
feeds off himself, off no one else but himself. His
plan, his becoming-other, just does not come about.
His time stands still in the repeated moment of the
failure to eat. "Glad to be unseen by everyone,"
"he enters a state of insignificance," like De
Certeau's dying man. Editors refuse his work, few
people enter the sphere of his monologue.
We need to clarify why Hamsun's *Hunger* is relevant
to us, leaving aside the linear connections that we
started with, along which we are developing this
train of thought and giving this essay its title.
Why inhibit digestion ex-ante, denying the
movement of the process of taking possession
of a context, even before denying its alteration or
transformation? Why does Filarete's column no
longer seem equal to the task of holding up the
world, "useful" for continuing a discourse? Why do
we believe that the landscape of waste, as well as
landscapes in general, need to be "treated" leaving
aside relationality and a project of appropriation,
a project that takes possession necessarily by
relating, and by taking possession attributes *itself*
(tasks, needs, uses) and attributes to the Other
(values, hierarchies, directions)? Why do we
accept our metaphorical digestion's distinction
in elements while refusing its synthesis, its
defecation without accepting the linearity of
the process that produces it?

And it is precisely here, in the difficulty
of "foreseeing" a possible use for that column
that *our* process comes to a halt, that we block our
digestion, to which we dedicate these reflections,
without any desire, as mentioned above, to imagine
for it (a trope of our reasoning) a regurgitation,
without wishing to expel it because it is
insignificant. That column could possibly remain
there, without being re-designed, projected towards
new proximities or new distances, whether physical
or temporal. What are its ties with its surroundings?
Hamsun's ties: the ties of someone who agreed not
to have ties, to attempt not to take over a context,
a food, experiencing this isolation, this "well-being
of isolation" in complete reciprocity, "untouched
by everything around [him]."
Maybe only an element that is left *alone* is capable
of resisting the shock of the unforeseeable: if only
because in that way—the height of selfishness
and/or arrogant selflessness—it can avoid involving
its neighbour in its own possible/inevitable process
of death (and given that it would be utopian
to imagine moving away, we are forced to remain
in a perspective of what is *useful*). Only an element
that is left without a project (without projections
towards someone, something, a relationship,
a sharing) is capable of accepting variations,
differences.
We have basically discussed the alteration
of a programme, of setbacks during the process
of prevision, prediction; we included the excerpt
concerning Filarete's column. It is this, this *being
precarious*, that shakes to the foundations the very
possibility of pursuing that "Western attitude
whereby 'there is always something to do'"
described above. It is the ever-possible alteration
of our forecasts, the instability of the contexts,
of what appears edible today in the world but may
no longer be so tomorrow[13] that makes the
usefulness, the *outcome* of that column uncertain.
Meaning that if we cannot accept it as being
useless, we must overcome our need to imagine
it as being useful "to someone" (to a project,
contained in a whole). This means leaving behind
the relational aspect in landscape planning.
Relations cannot come into being where the
instability of the interlocutor "makes it impossible"
to imagine a shared management of space,

11 March 1986, Fukushima (Japan)

THE MOST GROUNDBREAKING
CONSTRUCTING METHODS
KNOWN BY MAN
HAVE CLEARLY A
SHORTER DURATION
THAN THE NUCLEAR WASTE
THAT SHOULD BE
CONTAINED IN THEM

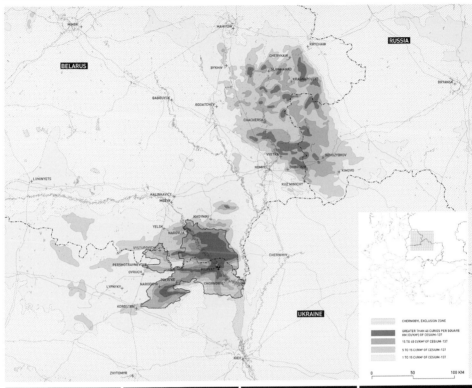

Map legend:

- CHERNOBYL EXCLUSION ZONE
- GREATER THAN 40 CURIES PER SQUARE KM (CI/KM²) OF CESIUM-137
- 15 TO 40 CI/KM² OF CESIUM-137
- 5 TO 15 CI/KM² OF CESIUM-137
- 1 TO 15 CI/KM² OF CESIUM-137

0   50   100 KM

Countries/places labeled on map: BELARUS, RUSSIA, UKRAINE, MINSK, MAHYOW, KRYCHAW, BRYANSK, CHERYKAW, SLAWHARAD, KRASNAPOLLIE, BYKHIV, BABRUJSK, ROGATCHEV, CHACHERSK, VYETKA, NOVOZYBKOV, HOMYEL, DOBRUSH, KIMOVO, KUZMINICHY, LUNINYETS, KALINKAVICY, MOZYR, KHOYNIKI, YELSK, NAROVLIA, VYSTUPOVICHY, PERSHOTRAVNEVYE, OVRUCH, POLESKE, CHORNOBYL, LYPNYKY, NARODYCHI, KOROSTEN, CHERNIHIV, KIEV, ZHYTOMYR

 A

AGRICOLTURAL LAND RE-APPROPRIATION

After the Chernobyl Accident, the land has been contaminated with radiation and has not been cultivated for 21 years.

One of the most challenging goals is to start to re-use the contaminated land to take and take advantage of the huge lands, once upon a time, used as agricultural land.

The concentration of Cesium-137 and Strontio-90 in the soil doesn't allow food production but the land could be used to produce bio fuel and bio gas.

The Agrarian University started a pilot project in Narodichi, a village on the west side of the Ukraine exclusion zone, where they used oilseed as a bio-remediation to attract it in vesements and to clean the soil.

We use this example to start design an agricultural park for bio fuel production and to speed up the radioactive decay.

 P

VILLAGES QUALITY OF LIFE IMPROVEMENT

Today in Belarus, Russia and Ukraine about 4.5 million of people live in contaminated land. The information about the number of deaths and the number of people suffering for the consequences of the Chernobyl incident are quite discordant. The situation is tough not only for the lack of money but also because of the bad way of living in this areas.

Usually the villages are small, about 300 people each. The common house is a small wood or brick building with one floor and a tiny and long band of garden on the back.

We plan to create micro actions to integrate the radioactive zones and, if necessary, devising a new sustainable residential areas to supply the manpower demand for the new agricultural farms.

T

TURISM DEVELOPMENT

Since 2002, the year it opened for visits, the trend of organised tours inside the zone raised constantly. One-day group excursions cost from $100 to $400 per person, including transportation and a meal, considering the Ukraine monthly salary, this is a huge amount of money and this is the reason why after 25 years the Ukraine government nationalized this business.

The main recent points for tourists are situated in ukraine, around the power plant in Pripyat. Today a tour inside the zone is allow paid with an ukrainian visitor only after have got a special authorisation.

We are planning to re-organise the tour with services and facilities to increase the visits and revitalise the surrounding villages.

E

ECOLOGICAL RESERVE CREATION

Currently, the area surrounding the power plant is an empty fenced space where it is not possible to get in without an authorisation. The land is abandoned and some animals are coming back because there are no human activity. Some researches show that the biodiversity is decreasing but others are much more optimistic about the future inside the zone, almost all are taking advantage of this unique situation where, for almost 25 years no one used this contaminated land.

The creation of an isolated radiologic reserve is a necessity which can hide an important potential from the research point of view. This empty land can became a huge laboratory to analyze the impact and the consequences of the nuclear radiations on the ecosystem, on the flora and fauna.

The idea is to reinforce the border of this area by creating a strong know element to forbid the entrance and to create a symbolic sign.

115

or an interlocution space. This results in the withdrawal of the project, its withdrawal from time and space, a concept described in greater detail below with the support of further arguments. A withdrawal from projection towards the Other in order to appropriate it, feed off it: thus leaving it *free*. A withdrawal from projection towards a Tomorrow, since it is only a by-product of that tomorrow, allowing it to *become*. But what happens in that isolation, what landscape is produced by these "withdrawals"? Maybe it is the withdrawal of the "power of prevision" that does not foresee, the "ambitious palace of this Milanese lord" that comes to a halt when faced with a becoming that it was unable to control, with surroundings that it was unable to appropriate, with a space that it no longer expanded into. Maybe it is the landscape of those "humble houses" that fortuitously *encounter* that column, rather than conquering it. With the same lack of premeditation as Hamsun's protagonist, who reached the port by chance. With the same detachment expressed in his request to embark, in a completely uncathartic finale, "utterly indifferent as to whether I was met by a refusal or not."

• • •

"Why should we live with such hurry and waste of life? We are determined to be starved before we are hungry."[14]

• • •

One of the possibilities emphasized by this essay from the outset concerned the possibility of preventive planning in landscape planning,[15] of anticipating the waste that the project itself proposes, save the possibility of stripping it of its relations, on the one hand, and consequently (if, as we have done, "the relationship" is considered in terms of "appropriation"), the opportunity of subtracting the "project thought" from the sphere of influence of determinism, that still somehow possesses it, separating the question of utility from the concept of "need": basically, by eliminating the idea that

the project must of necessity be useful, that a *project utility*, whatever this might be, will always exist—that it must always exist. We believe such operations are only credible if we accept the unforeseeability, introduced directly from other disciplines, of thinking "landscapes," also in an "architectural" rationale. A prevision immediately laying down the condition that its failure is the only thing capable of protecting it in the face of uncertainty, indeterminacy: a condition of this type can but mean accepting chance and therefore the chance of one's own end. But all in all, we end up getting trapped in a vicious circle: we said that we were unable to "premeditate" and that at the same time we need to foresee: in this context we simply foresee the need for precautions. That is, rather then projecting visions, we are projecting options, options capable of redefining themselves. Maybe we are proposing *antecedences* rather than previsions. How can foreseeing crises, establishing the end of the project as anteceding the project itself, be linked to the absence of relations and their subtraction? It is precisely the awareness of the possibility of waste that implies the exclusion of a systemic reasoning, that demands fractioning, incoherence, the absence of every type of *dependence*: abiding with the idea of *useful*, we should remember that no matter how autonomous the underlying framework is, once a part is inscribed in a structure its difficulties can compromise more than just itself. At the same time, leaving that idea aside, the exercise of power by a project—a concept examined in greater detail below—that goes beyond merely drawing attention to inequalities (between itself and the Other), and therefore distinguishing parts, must eliminate itself in that it is an appropriation of an elsewhere: of a space or time that are not its own. A Preventive Landscape must restore project functions of prevision, interpretation and guidance of the becoming, while putting forward strategies updated on the basis of the changed context, of the changing contexts, of tensions and drifts, in order to bring about an open, non-preclusive control of transformations. A Preventive Landscape makes indeterminacy its background and field of action, marked by the end of all certainties, and as a complex system where the project is called upon to perform its action of distinction, that is capable of assuming ex-ante its own potential critical areas, modifications of real and its significations, the transformations in the values and capacities of contexts, both physical and cultural. It is not a question of projecting into the becoming forms that are flexible enough to accept the unforeseeable, but strategies that assume it as its guiding force. Strategies that premise their own crisis resolving it in advance within their own frameworks. In this, what we cited as the consolidated "planning technique" of landscape design—that is, relational strategy, which is undoubtedly still valid in part—is experiencing some difficulties as far as its "holding capacity" is concerned. A logical node, in fact, seems to interrupt its effectiveness as soon as it faces the discontinuity that has become the symbol of our times, and to which everybody has to adapt; a discontinuity that can but shatter any form of complexity aspiring to be systemic. Certainly, from a *cultural* perspective—where "culture" means a set of interrelated knowledge and notions, such as all of the values, traditions, and customs characterizing a civilization—relational thinking is still necessary when dealing with landscape, if we are to grasp all of its specificities. However, if we consider the practice actually implied by acting in a culture and we signify it as the ability to choose and select,[16] perhaps, in our approach to a context, we might use an attitude other than the relational, one which assumes the possibility of division, separation, digestion and, therefore, even the disposal of some parts, thus defining it with the necessary discontinuity between elements; that is, not only in its "actual" state but also in its becoming. The imposition of distinctions appears to be the only possible strategy for the formulation of a "system" that involves different degrees of intensity in terms of development and degrowth (going back to our triangle: along the two lines that go from *raw* to *putrid* either directly or indirectly through *cooked*), including the eventual replacement of some of its parts (a succession without ties), and that reasons using referenceless fragments, whereby the solution (dissolution)

of the nodes does not compromise the staticity or dynamics of the whole. Perhaps the only possible approach—when a project is aware of its unavoidable wear and tear, of the need to be a discharge/replacement process—is one that breaks relationships as a necessity, and structures the territory by fragments, awaiting what might become of each single part; awaiting perhaps the disposal of the prevision or its possible becoming-other. Perhaps, in conclusion, a separate project collection—an interdependence-based project even in the presence of manifest connections which are valid but cannot be generalized—is the only strategy allowing us to approach, in a sufficiently precautionary manner, the accidental arrangement of events, or the entropic movement of a territory that is "becoming."

• • •

"This is not an issue of antitheater, of theater in the theater, or of theater denying the theater, etc.: Carmelo Bene is disgusted by so-called avant-garde formulas. It is a matter of a more precise operation: you begin by subtracting, deducting everything that would constitute an element of power, in language and in gestures, in the representation and in the represented. You cannot even say that it is a negative operation because it already enlists and releases positive processes. You will then deduct or amputate history because History is the temporal marker of Power. You will subtract structure because it is the synchronic marker, the totality of relations among invariants. You will subtract constants, the stable or stabilized elements, because they belong to major usage. You will amputate the text because the text is like the domination of language over speech and still attests to invariance or homogeneity. You deduct dialogue because it transmits elements of power into speech and causes them to spread: it is your turn to speak under such codified conditions [...]. But what remains? Everything remains, but under a new light with new sounds and new gestures."[17]

• • •

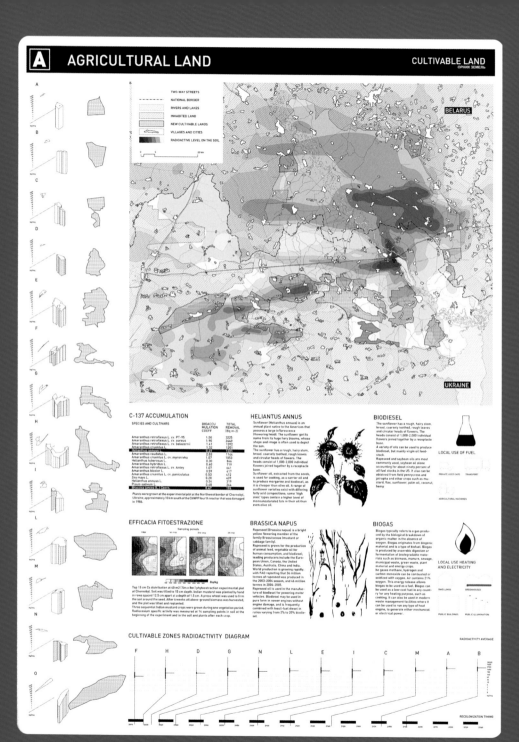

Legend:
- TWO-WAY STREETS
- NATIONAL BORDER
- RIVERS AND LAKES
- INHABITED LAND
- NEW CULTIVABLE LANDS
- VILLAGES AND CITIES
- RADIOACTIVE LEVEL ON THE SOIL

BELARUS

UKRAINE

C-137 ACCUMULATION

SPECIES AND CULTIVARS	BIOACCUMULATION COEFF	TOTAL REMOVAL [Bq m-2]
Amaranthus retroflexus L. cv. PT-95	1.56	3225
Amaranthus retroflexus L. cv. aureus	1.90	2440
Amaranthus retroflexus L. cv. belozernii	1.41	1392
Amaranthus cruentus L.	1.32	1261
Helianthus annuus L.	0.93	1275
Amaranthus caudatus L.	2.03	1166
Amaranthus cruentus L. cv. myronivka	1.07	1053
Helianthus tuberosus L.	0.30	846
Amaranthus hybridus L.	0.60	719
Amaranthus cruentus L. cv. Antey	1.07	641
Amaranthus bicolor L.	0.59	417
Amaranthus cruentus L. cv. paniculatus	0.53	412
Zea mays L.	0.28	409
Helianthus annuus L.	0.24	319
Pisum sativum L.	0.48	244
Brassica juncea (L.) Czern.	0.47	143

Plants were grown at the experimental plot at the Northwest border of Chernobyl, Ukraine, approximately 10km south of the ChNPP fourth reactor that was damaged in 1986.

HELIANTUS ANNUS

Sunflower (Helianthus annuus) is an annual plant native to the Americas that possess a large inflorescence (flowering head). The sunflower got its name from its huge fiery blooms, whose shape and image is often used to depict the sun.

The sunflower has a rough, hairy stem, broad, coarsely toothed, rough leaves and circular heads of flowers. The heads consist of 1,000–2,000 individual flowers joined together by a receptacle base.

Sunflower oil, extracted from the seeds, is used for cooking, as a carrier oil and to produce margarine and biodiesel, as it is cheaper than olive oil. A range of sunflower varieties exist with differing fatty acid compositions, some 'high oleic' types contain a higher level of monounsaturated fats in their oil than even olive oil.

BIODIESEL

The sunflower has a rough, hairy stem, broad, coarsely toothed, rough leaves and circular heads of flowers. The heads consist of 1,000–2,000 individual flowers joined together by a receptacle base.

A variety of oils can be used to produce biodiesel, but mainly virgin oil feedstock.

Rapeseed and soybean oils are most commonly used, soybean oil alone accounting for about ninety percent of all fuel stocks in the US. It also can be obtained from field pennycress and jatropha and other crops such as mustard, flax, sunflower, palm oil, coconut, hemp.

LOCAL USE OF FUEL

PRIVATE USED CARS   TRANSPORT

AGRICULTURAL MACHINES

EFFICACIA FITOESTRAZIONE

Sampling periods

Bq/kg

Top 15 cm Cs distribution at 60 m2 l 5m x 8m l phytoextraction experimental plot at Chernobyl. Soil was tilled to 15 cm depth. Indian mustard was planted by hand in rows spaced 12.5 cm apart at a depth of 1.5 cm. A press wheel was used to firm the soil around the seed. After 6 weeks all above-ground biomass was harvested, and the plot was tilled and replanted.

Three sequential Indian mustard crops were grown during one vegetation period. Radiocesium specific activity was measured at 14 sampling points in soil at the beginning of the experiment and in the soil and plants after each crop.

BRASSICA NAPUS

Rapeseed (Brassica napus) is a bright yellow flowering member of the family Brassicaceae (mustard or cabbage family).

Rapeseed is grown for the production of animal feed, vegetable oil for human consumption, and biodiesel; leading producers include the European Union, Canada, the United States, Australia, China and India. World production is growing rapidly, with FAO reporting that 36 million tonnes of rapeseed was produced in the 2003–2004 season, and 46 million tonnes in 2004–2005.

Rapeseed oil is used in the manufacture of biodiesel for powering motor vehicles. Biodiesel may be used in pure form in newer engines without engine damage, and is frequently combined with fossil-fuel diesel in ratios varying from 2% to 20% biodiesel.

BIOGAS

Biogas typically refers to a gas produced by the biological breakdown of organic matter in the absence of oxygen. Biogas originates from biogenic material and is a type of biofuel. Biogas is produced by anaerobic digestion or fermentation of biodegradable materials such as biomass, manure, sewage, municipal waste, green waste, plant material and energy crops.

he gases methane, hydrogen and carbon monoxide can be combusted or oxidized with oxygen. Air contains 21% oxygen. This energy release allows biogas to be used as a fuel. Biogas can be used as a low-cost fuel in any country for any heating purpose, such as cooking. It can also be used in modern waste management facilities where it can be used to run any type of heat engine, to generate either mechanical or electrical power.

LOCAL USE HEATING AND ELECTRICITY

DWELLINGS   GREENHOUSES

PUBLIC BUILDINGS   PUBLIC ILLUMINATION

CULTIVABLE ZONES RADIOACTIVITY DIAGRAM

RADIOACTIVITY AVERAGE

F   H   D   G   N   L   E   I   C   M   A   B

RECOLONIZATION TIMING

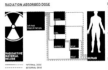

RESIDENT POPULATION

RADIATION ABSORBED DOSE

RADIOACTIVE MATERIAL RELEASE — AIR AND PRECIPITATION — ANIMALS — HUMAN

INTERNAL DOSE
EXTERNAL DOSE

Legend

- TWO-WAY STREETS
- NATIONAL BORDER
- RIVERS AND LAKES
- INHABITED LAND
- NEW COLTIVABLE AREAS
- VILLAGES AND CITIES OUTSIDE THE ZONE
- INHABITED VILLAGES INSIDE THE ZONE
- EVACUATED VILLAGES INSIDE THE ZONE
- NEW VILLAGES DEVELOPMENT

BELARUS

UKRAINE

VEGETABLE CONTAMINATION LEVEL

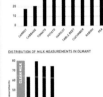

% TO PEA — CARROT, CABBAGE, TOMATO, POTATO, HARICOT, TABLE BEET, CUCUMBER, RADISH, PEA

DISTRIBUTION OF MILK MEASUREMENTS IN OLMANY

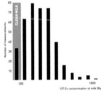

CLEAN MILK

Number of measurements

137 Cs contamination of milk (Bq/l)

RESULTS OF MEASUREMENTS OF CONTAMINATED ASHES

100R–150R, 500R–550R, 10–50R, 1K–15K

REGULATORY LIMIT

Number of measurements

DOSE CONTRIBUTION

INTERNAL – FISH INGESTION
EXTERNAL – SHORE
INTERNAL – FOOD INGESTION
INTERNAL – WATER DRINKING
EXTERNAL – SMOKING
EXTERNAL – SOIL

MEASURED AMBIENT DOSE RATES

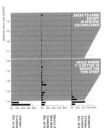

Ambient dose rate (μSv/h)

AREAS TO AVOID EXCEPT IN SPECIFIC CIRCUMSTANCE

AREAS WHERE IT IS BETTER TO REDUCE THE TIME SPENT

DISTRIBUTION OF THE MEASUREMENTS PERFORMED INSIDE HOUSES

DISTRIBUTION OF THE MEASUREMENTS PERFORMED NEAR AND INSIDE STORES

DISTRIBUTION OF THE MEASUREMENTS PERFORMED IN PRIVATE GARDENS

VILLAGES POPULATED OUTSIDE THE ZONE

FOOD PROBLEMS

The reality of the contamination, in the affected areas, is linked, directly, to food. 70-90% of the radiations (resulting from the cesium 137, strontium 90 and in part by Plutonium) passes Directly from the soil to food and from food to living beings.

HUMUS PROJECT

Represents an example of international cooperation, with social and agricultural facets, intended for the people of Belarus affected by the nuclear disaster of Chernobyl.
The project provides guidelines exportable to other similar situations in which devastation by contamination or environmental disasters is involving, first of all, the Food.

OBJECTIVES

Social dimension: construction of pedagogical / cultural references to the "food risk" by involving the whole population of a village highly exposed to contamination.

Agricultural dimension: plans for the construction of greenhouses for production, within the contaminated area, of different crops all this without use of contaminated terrain thanks to the adopting of the techniques of "substrate" and eating system.

THE GLASSHOUSE OF MOLCIANY

The Sovchoz of Molciany is located 15 km south-west of Recitza (in the Gomel region), currently 350 people live there (counting about 100 households).
The Sovchoz is now called "Istok" (The Source) and the greenhouse, it hosts, has an area of 1 hectare and it's glass and metal structure is capable of providing an internal temperature of +15° when outside, the temperature, is -35°.

People involved:
1 Administrative Director
An agronomist
1 warehouse responsible
15 workers
4 maintenance workers
A beekeeper
3 guards
Salary: $ 40 per month

Data: (cucumber cultivation 2004)
Nitrate: 189 mg / kg
Radionuclides: cesium137 2.5 Bq / kg
Pesticides: none
Lead: none
Arsenic: none
Mercury: none
The content of cesium137 does not exceed legal limits (RDU 99).

AGRICULTURAL TECHNOLOGY

Plans for the construction of greenhouses for production, within the contaminated area, of different crops all this without use of contaminated terrain thanks to the adopting of the techniques of "substrate" and eating system.

SUBSTRATE

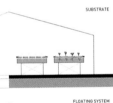

FLOATING SYSTEM

ACQUAPHONICA

VILLAGES INHABITED INSIDE THE ZONE

The situation of the populated villages within the zone is under constant monitoring. Data from 2002 shows a significant decrease of population due to aging.
It is reasonable to assume that in a short time, these villages will be completely uninhabited.

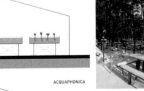

1-5, 5-10, 10-15, 15-30, 30-100, 100-300

GHOST VILLAGES

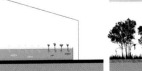

Earlier we put forward the hypothesis of the project's withdrawal from time and space. It withdraws from time by proposing itself as if it had an "expiry date," as if it were preemptively aware of its end; pro-posing itself not as "continuous" but, rather, as distinct, broken down into subsequent phases. It withdraws from space by halting at the threshold of the Other, almost forcing itself to suffer hunger: digestion, as we said, is a project of appropriation. We have underlined how these hypotheses can be useful, but at the same time we have also stressed the need to break free from a "usefulness-centred" way of thinking. On the one hand, the impossibility of "indicating tasks" within the "society of uncertainty" leads to the tendency to freeze hypotheses in time, on the basis of considerations of mere opportunity, and to the use of the conditional; on the other hand, it limits expansion and relationships with surroundings, with the risk of spreading unpredictabilities, a chain of crises. We linked the difficulty involved in considering a new use for the column (our trope, we repeat) to abundant recourse to *evacuation* on the part of modernity, the overabundance of waste in local territories; or, again with regard to reactions, the success of the recycling strategy (recycling of both meaning and matter): a strategy still connected to the idea of usefulness, and therefore still somehow linked to a teleological, finalistic principle, which always entails the need for a stated purpose (of the actions and products). In our opinion, recycling is a guiding principle that is hardly in line with what other disciplines indicate to be a phenomenological emergency; Heisenberg's indetermination in short.[18] We have opposed our "separate collection" strategy to all of this: a generative decomposition which releases actions without indicating tasks. Now we would like to enrich this strategy with reasons, with a final consideration that somehow attempts to abandon the realm of the useful, perhaps by *de facto* crossing a boundary into the field of ethics. This consideration also relates to the concept of "preventive," even though it is centred on that of "power": this withdrawal from previsions and relationships is a withdrawal of the Power of the project, its exploiting and feeding on the Other, whether it be space or time.

Everything is based on the concept of "minor," as opposed to "major," introduced by Deleuze in his comment on Carmelo Bene's work.[19] Indeed, a continuous incremental development can only have augmentative effects on the stock of waste which we will increasingly have to deal with: the immediate evidence of the advantage of a "reductive" approach, in terms of quantity, can but meld perfectly with our preventive strategy. However, in this particular context reduction is not just "wanted" for these effects, which are as ever linked to the useful. Here the meaning given to it by Deleuze is fully embraced: reduction as a form of *liberation*. The relational rule, as we said, lives out of principle; similarly, and as directly, when "making landscapes" basically only one operation is applied: an increase in quantity, an elevation to a cultural "more," the superimposition of a signifier. Regardless of the extent to which it simplifies things or acts by subtraction, a project necessarily triggers and designs its own perspective, even when this entails a regression or deadlock. Although increasingly accompanying rather than guiding in its pursuit and seconding of the present, a project always represents an exercise of power, even when its control is ineffective. The project's power is one of inexorably producing "landscape," even unwittingly, unintentionally. It replaces reality with a new epic, updates or reiterates the existing ones.
So how, and, above all, *why,* should we keep a project from making landscapes? The point is to define the ways in which a project intervenes, and the degree of power it exercises. Because, even if our words ("withdrawal," "prevention," "separate collection") place us in the area of *activities* carried out upon a context, when planning, we have to decide to what extent we want to leave that context passive or, conversely, to release it and leave it *active*. If, in short, we imagine and prefigure a *direction* for a context, it is a matter of understanding in what way and to what extent this is possible and, even before that, if this is legitimate and worthwhile: *leaving a transformation to be what it is*; leaving our "humble houses" to be what they are. Bene lets Horatio have Hamlet's monologue. In the same way, Deleuze observes, Mercutio passes away early in Shakespeare, while he does not want to die

with Bene. Not just for the sake of altering a story: it is rather to oppose the *recital* of History, its repeating itself always identically or similarly, everywhere. It is to oppose the umpteenth *interpretation*. This, after all, is the starting point: interpreting a place, designing a landscape, means magnifying it just as in the reruns of Shakespeare's plays. This magnification, however, is carried out by increasing the "flavour" where it already holds some value, or by making it an acquired taste: the landscape receiving the project grows *bigger*, becomes *normalized*. It is *normal*, or at least it was until Laforgue, if not until Carmelo Bene, to *interpret* Hamlet in the way Shakespeare portrayed him and, therefore, consigned him to History. Likewise, it is *normal* to *interpret* the project as a form of "control," appropriation, power over the Other. The same thing happens to the Apulian peasants, recalls Deleuze, after they were given "culture" (cinema, theatre, television), after they were made "major," they were somehow "normalized." Bene uses a rather different approach, subtracting something from the original work: in other words, *Un Amleto di meno*. He does not use addition, but subtraction, reduction. This is the operation carried out on Shakespeare (regardless of what the subtracted element is). Likewise, we can imagine excluding some aspects of our project. We will no longer process its power in terms of slavish reproduction or updating, but rather aim for its degeneration, its transformation into something that is non-standard. Then, if our association works—if theatre and acting practice is the same as project practice, we can translate into our field the operation carried out by Bene, thus making it valid in the *body* of territories as it was in the body of the actor. Still we are left with the task of understanding what to subtract and *how*. Bene's *Hamlet* consists of a continuous failure to meet expectations: filial duties avoided, the coherence of a role denied, and the shirking of one's role, one's specificity, one's institutional character. Some monologues are truncated, while some dialogues become monologues.

Likewise, the degeneration of his *Richard III*, his becoming deformed, is the degeneration of power, a loss of words whose aim is not to keep silent, but rather to say something different and trigger a new discourse which will appear fragmentary and incoherent to those tied to the old meaning, to History as it was handed down. The object of subtraction is passiveness: the passiveness of the acting that *suffers* the original text and plays up to it; and the passiveness of the text that *suffers* the acting, which is reiterated again and again. Then we perhaps might use the lever of the power of codification (codification of roles, relationships), reducing its level and scope, paying new attention to neglected space, to secondary events. Some protagonists will no longer predominate and some extras will remain on stage longer than expected. It will mean removing codified hierarchies, the internal coherence of a character, the relationships between actors, and the pre-written dialogue. No longer repeating oneself as relational in time and space: perhaps secluding oneself in Hamsun's *Hunger*, or in Huysman's Fontenay-aux-Roses, regardless of the different relationships that will be spontaneously recreated. Mies' step backward in his *Seagram*[20] is the subtraction of a relationship created and established by Manhattan's grid with the aim of releasing new ones. Matta-Clark's cuts in *Bingo* simply eliminate past connections to establish new ones. "Relationality" is the power to reduce. Like *Un Amleto di meno*, the landscaping project should cause its role to degenerate, breaking free from the rule that compares it to a dialogue in which everyone reads their lines according to the script. "Pro-jecting" is the power to reduce: if the project is no longer projective and *meaningful*, it becomes a subtraction and may allow things *to be said* in a different manner, transformed by in experience from what was imagined, from what was staged in the past: Mercutio will constitute the new play. Removing the power of relations, of planning, is anything but normal: it represents a degeneration of practice as well as a possibility of thus rendering the original text and the actor truly active elements. It will mean amputating hierarchy, subsequence, History, and logic; subtracting the stable elements, the *major* context of the real. It will mean disregarding every meaning, determination, and institutional character. No forced regression or progression; just active

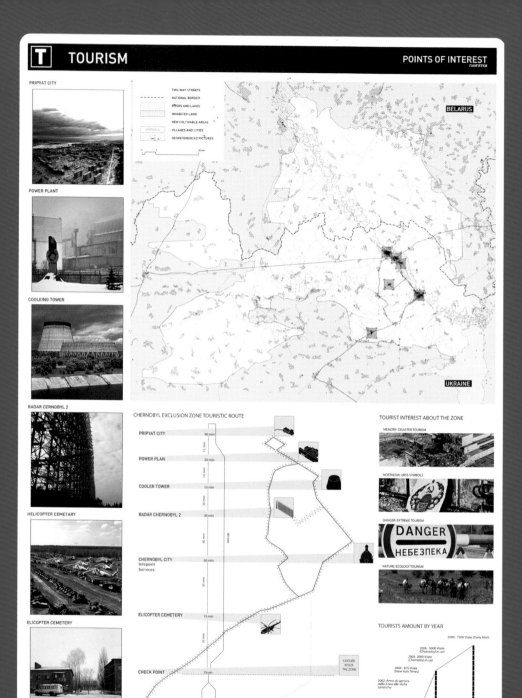

PRIPYAT CITY

POWER PLANT

COOLEING TOWER

RADAR CERNOBYL 2

HELICOPTER CEMETARY

ELICOPTER CEMETERY

TWO-WAY STREETS
NATIONAL BORDER
RIVERS AND LAKES
INHABITED LAND
NEW COLTIVABLE AREAS
VILLAGES AND CITIES
GEOREFERENCED PICTURES

BELARUS

UKRAINE

CHERNOBYL EXCLUSION ZONE TOURISTIC ROUTE

PRIPYAT CITY — 90 min
POWER PLAN — 20 min
COOLER TOWER — 10 min
RADAR CHERNOBYL 2 — 30 min
CHERNOBYL CITY — 60 min
Infopoint
Services
ELICOPTER CEMETERY — 15 min
CHECK POINT — 15min

IVANKYV, KYIV

Old turistic route

TOURIST INTEREST ABOUT THE ZONE

MEMORY: DISASTER TOURISM

NOSTALGIA: URSS SYMBOLS

DANGER: EXTREME TOURISM

DANGER
НЕБЕЗПЕКА

NATURE: ECOLOGY TOURISM

TOURISTS AMOUNT BY YEAR

2009 : 7500 Visite (Daily Mail)
2006 : 5000 Visite (Chornobyl.in.ua)
2005 : 2000 Visite (Chornobyl.in.ua)
2004 : 870 Visite (New York Times)
2002: Anno di apertura della Zona alle visite turistiche

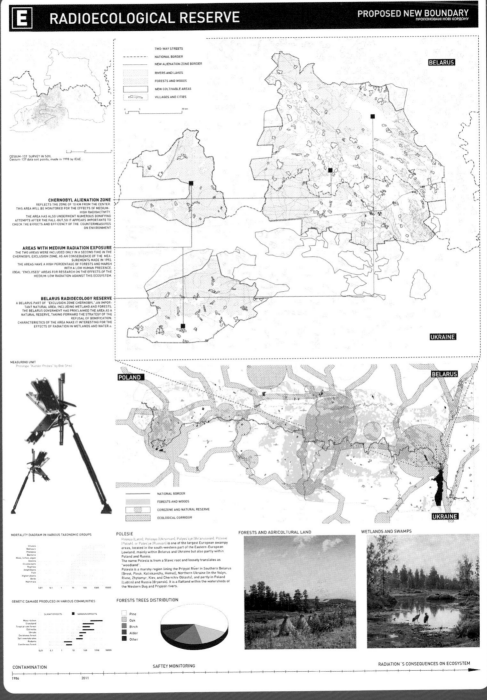

RADIOECOLOGICAL RESERVE

PROPOSED NEW BOUNDARY
ПРОПОНОВАНІ НОВІ КОРДОНУ

E

BELARUS

UKRAINE

POLAND

BELARUS

UKRAINE

TWO-WAY STREETS
NATIONAL BORDER
NEW ALIENATION ZONE BORDER
RIVERS AND LAKES
FORESTS AND WOODS
NEW COLTIVABLE AREAS
VILLAGES AND CITIES

CESIUM-137 SURVEY IN SOIL
Cesium-137 data soil points, made in 1998 by IEAE .

CHERNOBYL ALIENATION ZONE
REFLECTS THE ZONE OF 10 KM FROM THE CENTER.
THIS AREA WILL BE MONITORED FOR THE EFFECTS OF MEDIUM-HIGH RADIOACTIVITY.
THE AREA HAS ALSO UNDERWENT NUMEROUS BONIFYING ATTEMPTS AFTER THE FALL-OUT,SO IT APPEARS IMPORTANTE TO CHECK THE EFFECTS AND EFFICENCY OF THE COUNTERMEASURES ON ENVIRONMENT

AREAS WITH MEDIUM RADIATION EXPOSURE
THE TWO AREAS WERE INCLUDED ONLY IN A SECOND TIME IN THE CHERNOBYL EXCLUSION ZONE, AS AN CONSEQUENCE OF THE MEASUREMENTS MADE IN 1992.
THE AREAS HAVE A HIGH PERCENTAGE OF FORESTS AND MARSH WITH A LOW HUMAN PRECENCE.
IDEAL "ENCLOSED" AREAS FOR RESEARCH ON THE EFFECTS OF THE MEDIUM-LOW RADIATION AGAINST THIS ECOSYSTEM.

BELARUS RADIOECOLOGY RESERVE
A BELARUS PART OF "EXCLUSION ZONE CHERNOBYL" AN IMPORTANT NATURAL AREA, INCLUDING WETLAND AND FORESTS.
THE BELARUS GOVERMENT HAS PROCLAIMED THE AREA AS A NATURAL RESERVE,TAKING FORWARD THE STRATEGY OF THE REFUSAL OF BONIFICATION.
CHARACTERISTICS OF THE AREA MAKE IT INTERESTING FOR THE EFFECTS OF RADIATION IN WETLANDS AND WATER.s

MEASURING UNIT
Prototype "Kielder Probes" by Biel Shoi

NATIONAL BORDER
FORESTS AND WOODS
COREZONE AND NATURAL RESERVE
ECOLOGICAL CORRIDOR

POLESIE
Polesie (Latin), Polissya (Ukrainian), Palyes'ye (Belarussian), Polesie (Polish), or Poles'ye (Russian) is one of the largest European swampy areas, located in the south-western part of the Eastern-European Lowland, mainly within Belarus and Ukraine but also partly within Poland and Russia.
The name Polesia is from a Slavic root and loosely translates as "woodland".
Polesia is a marshy region lining the Pripyat River in Southern Belarus (Brest, Pinsk, Kalinkavichy, Homel), Northern Ukraine (in the Volyn, Rivne, Zhytomyr, Kiev, and Chernihiv Oblasts), and partly in Poland (Lublin) and Russia (Bryansk). It is a flatland within the watersheds of the Western Bug and Prypyat rivers.

MORTALITY DIAGRAM IN VARIOUS TAXONOMIC GROUPS

GENETIC DAMAGE PRODUCED IN VARIOUS COMMUNITIES

FORESTS TREES DISTRIBUTION
Pine
Oak
Birch
Alder
Other

FORESTS AND AGRICOLTURAL LAND

WETLANDS AND SWAMPS

CONTAMINATION   SAFTEY MONITORING   RADIATION´S CONSEQUENCES ON ECOSYSTEM

1986   2011

unpredictability against passive reciprocal control; a removal that may only make it possible to focus on one detail that consequently acquires new life; making it possible to overturn habits: "I appeared to the Virgin Mary," as Bene said…
By separating and, therefore, also by discarding things, according to a rationale of discontinuity between elements, the original work may perhaps "vacillate; it will spin, it will lean on a different side": not a new interpretation, but rather a new level of understanding. It will no longer be the habit of re-reading given relationships, the respect of hierarchies, of *antecedences* that are *precedences*: it will be the liberation of a disconnected movement, which is out of control but alive. It may mean monologues, the Artaudian destruction of the language, but no pre-scribed dialogues. The landscaping project will no longer impose any *culture* on the Apulian peasants; the only culture it will employ for the landscape

is the choice of not proposing those features that are capable of making it "major."

• • •

This is how we will resolve our initial words, this is how they will become our *Digestions*, our separate project collection: an *alteration* which lives through *reduction*; a reduction that cuts off relationships and connections; the subtraction of the Power, which stops being exercised through *appropriation*; the subtraction of *dependence*, resolved by separating parts that can be allied but no longer hierarchical or interrelated; the subtraction of the primary role, of any *antecedence*; the subtraction of the *irreversibility* of *choices*; the subtraction, finally, of *secrecy*, which is nothing but the disclosure of differences, the rejection of any normalization, the acceptance of the deformities of Richard III' and of each *Landscape of Waste*.

[1] "In my restaurant self-organizing systems do not only feed upon order, they will also find noise on the menu," Heinz Von Foerster, *Understanding Understanding. Essays on Cybernetics and Cognition* (New York: Springer-Verlag, 2003), p. 11.
[2] Yve-Alain Bois and Rosalind Krauss, *Formless* (New York: Zone Books, 1997).
[3] Ludwig Feuerbach, *Die Geheimniss des Opfers oder der Mensch ist was er isst* (*The Mystery of Sacrifice or Man Is What He Eats*), 1862.
[4] "I'll teach you differences," says Wittgenstein drawing upon *King Lear*…
[5] Aldo Rossi, *A Scientific Autobiography*, trans. Lawrence Venuti (Cambridge, Mass.: MIT Press, 1984, p. 6.
[6] Michel de Certeau, *The Practice of Everyday Life* (*L'Invention du quotidien*, 1980), trans. Steven Rendall (Berkeley: University of California Press, 1984), pp. 190–91.
[7] Anthony Vidler, *The Architectural Uncanny. Essays in the Modern Unhomely* (Cambridge, Mass.: MIT Press, 1994).
[8] Knut Hamsun, *Hunger* (*Sult*, 1890), trans. George Egerton (New York: Courier Dover Publications, 2003).
[9] Günther Anders, *Die Antiquiertheit des Menschen* (1956) (Munich: Verlag C. H. Beck, 1995). Our translation.
[10] Nietzsche's *Wille zur Macht*: hunger as both creator and destroyer, as truth and its overcoming, as statement and denial; desire (of hunger) included in a relentless mechanism that constantly pursuits its own growth and, at the same time, endless drive for renovation, for its overcoming.
[11] "If one only had just a little to eat on such a lightsome day! The sense of the glad morning overwhelmed me; my satisfaction became ill-regulated, and for no definite reason I began to hum joyfully. At a butcher's stall a woman stood speculating on sausage for dinner. As I passed her she looked up at me. She had but one tooth in the front of her head. I had become so nervous and easily affected in the last few days that the woman's face made a loathsome impression upon me. The long yellow snag looked like a little finger pointing out of her gum, and her gaze was still

full of sausage as she turned it upon me. I immediately lost all appetite, and a feeling of nausea came over me," Knut Hamsun, *Hunger*. Here a comparison with the nausea and, above all, the isolation of the Des Esseintes of Huysmans would be not only possible, but interesting: see Joris-Karl Huysmans, *Against Nature* (*A rebours*, 1884), trans. Margaret Mauldon, edited by Nicholas White (Oxford: Oxford University Press, 1998).

[12] "I catch a glimpse of a man at the rail; the red lantern slung at the port shines down upon his head, and I get up and talk over to him. I had no object in talking, as I did not expect to get a reply, either. I said: 'Do you sail tonight, Captain?' 'Yes; in a short time,' answered the man. He spoke Swedish. 'Hem, I suppose you wouldn't happen to need a man?' I was at this instant utterly indifferent as to whether I was met by a refusal or not; it was all the same to me what reply the man gave me, so I stood and waited for it," Knut Hamsun, *Hunger*.

[13] From *Bovine Spongiform Encephalopathy*, to *H5N1*, *Swine influenza virus*, and *Escherichia Coli*, we could say...

[14] Henry David Thoreau, *Walden*, vol. 1 (Boston: Houghton, Mifflin and Company, 1854), p. 146.

[15] "Planning must become preventive rather than curative of social ills," Cedric Price, *The Square Book* (Chichester: Wiley

Academy, 2003), p. 38.

[16] "We all remember Claude Lévi-Strauss's assertion that the first 'cultural act' in history was the splitting of the population of females—however uniform they might be in their reproductive potential—into women eligible for sexual intercourse and those who were not. Culture is the activity of making distinctions: of classifying, segregating, drawing boundaries—and so dividing people into categories internally united by similarity and externally separated by difference; and of differentiating the ranges of conduct assigned to the humans allocated to different categories. As Frederich Barth famously pointed out, what culture defines as difference, a difference significant enough to justify the separation of categories, is the *product* of boundary-drawing, not its *cause* or motive," Zygmunt Bauman, *The Individualized Society* (Cambridge, UK: Polity Press, 2001), p. 32.

[17] Gilles Deleuze, *One Less Manifesto*, in Timothy Murray, ed., *Mimesis, Masochism, and Mime. The Politics of Theatricality in Contemporary French Thought* (*Un manifeste de moins*, 1979), trans. Eliane dal Molin and Timothy Murray (Ann Arbor: University of Michigan Press, 1997). See, among others, Ronald Bogue, *Deleuze on Literature* (New York and London: Routledge, 2003), Chapter 5.

[18] We still consider this to be

the approach structuring our reality. See, instead, the summary in *New Scientists* 2810, "End of Uncertainty" (30 April 2011); the same periodical, after all, entitled issue no. 2705 of 25 April 2009: "Goodbye Trash! Hello to a Future Fuelled by Vaporised Rubbish." In our opinion, this was definitely a premature hope...

[19] *One less Manifesto* echos *One Hamlet less* (*Un Amleto di meno*) by Carmelo Bene.

[20] "The absoluteness of the object is total here: the maximum absence of images corresponds to the maximum degree of formal structurality. This *language of absence* is projected towards a further 'void' which reflects the former and makes it resonate: the little city square that separates the skyscraper from Park Avenue [...] is not a place of rest and contemplation [...]. Rather, that city square is the planimetric overturning of the skyscraper's meaning: these two 'voids' refer to each other and speak the hallucinatory language of nothing and silence, which—a Kafkaesque paradox—'assaults' the noise of the metropolis. This double 'absent structure' withdraws from the city just as it exposes itself to it. Here renunciation, the classic *Entsagung*, is final. In order to enunciate it, *Mies takes a step backward and keeps silent*," Manfredo Tafuri, in Manfredo Tafuri and Francesco Dal Co, *Architettura contemporanea* (Milan: Electa, 1976), p. 307. Our translation.

Alberto Bertagna (1976), architect, PhD, Research Fellow at the University Iuav of Venice, taught at the University of Chieti-Pescara and at the University of Udine. He has published among others *Il controllo dell'indeterminato. Potëmkin villages e altri nonluoghi* (Macerata: Quodlibet, 2010) e *La città tragica. L'(an)architettura come (de)costruzione* (Reggio Emilia: Diabasis, 2006).

Renato Bocchi (1949), is Professor of Architectural and Urban Design at the University Iuav of Venice, Faculty of Architecture, where he directed the Architectural Design Department from 2006 to 2009 and coordinates today the research area and the degree course on Landscape Design. The main field of his research is the relationship between architecture, city and landscape. On this subject he coordinated (with E. Fontanari) in Venice the series of eight international conferences "Dessiner sur l'herbe" (2004–10). His most recent book: *Progettare lo spazio e il movimento* (Rome: Gangemi, 2009).

Giovanni Corbellini (1959), architect, PhD, critic of contemporary architecture, taught in Venice, Ferrara and Milan. He is currently Assistant Professor at the University of Trieste. Author of numerous publications, his recent essays are *Ex libris. 16 parole chiave dell'architettura contemporanea* (Milan: 22 publishing, 2007), *Bioreboot. The Architecture of R&Sie[n]* (Milan: 22 publishing – New York: Princeton Architectural Press, 2009), *Le pillole del dott. Corbellini* (Syracuse: LetteraVentidue, 2010).

Enrico Fontanari (1952), urban planner, Professor of Urban and Landscape Design and Planning at the University Iuav of Venice and in several international post-graduate programmes (Masters and PhD). Member of various international research teams in the fields of Urban and Landscape Design, is also consultant for many international agencies (United Nations, World Bank, European Union). Has more then thirty years of professional experience all over the world and is author of various publications on Urban and Landscape Design and Planning.

Sara Marini (1974), architect, PhD, lives and works in Venice. In 2008 she won the international fellowship "Research in Paris" launched by the City of Paris. Since 2010 is Assistant Professor in Architectural and Urban Design at the University Iuav of Venice. Among her recent publications: *Architettura parassita. Strategie di riciclaggio per la città* (Macerata: Quodlibet, 2008), *Nuove terre. Architetture e paesaggi dello scarto* (Macerata: Quodlibet, 2010).

Captions

pp. 12–21: Emmanuele Lo Giudice. *Renovatio Urbis Venetiarum 2010*. Graduation thesis, supervisors Renato Bocchi, Yona Friedman, Sara Marini, University Iuav of Venice, 2009–10.

Our civilization is formed by societies who collect memories, living a temporality of an exclusive privilege "of the present," in a spirit of immediate consumption in line with the dramatization of the world. This temporality of ours is unable to crystallize, in constant flight from the fragile reality of becoming time, in a continuous illusory utopia of eternal contemporaneity. Our age does not produce more time but rubble, glittering debris inside which an idea of the city survives in fragments. It lies within the rubble, waiting for a time in the making, a ruin that will not come again. It lies within this rubble, the contemporary form of utopia: the lost time of memory, which transforms things into relics to take home after the long journey of life. Everything becomes a sign and evidence, producing a unique form of archaeology. The city lives from this balance: a peaceful coexistence among different universes within a collective memory of a thousand possible cities, over the rubble of a time that will never become ruins, but stories, spaces, floors and fragments of other universes that are ever-more complex and layered. (E. Lo Giudice)

pp. 25–45: Giovanni Carli, Riccardo Miotto. *Waste/Transformations/Landscapes. Designing Scenarios for the Venice Lagoon*. Graduation thesis, supervisors Renato Bocchi, Enrico Fontanari, Sara Marini, University Iuav of Venice, 2009–10.

The work's main theme is the dissipative phenomena in natural and artificial ecosytems and the use of waste in landscape transformation processes. The project concerns Sacca San Mattia, a "dump-island" entirely made from glass waste from Murano and building refuse from Venice. The final solution adopts self-design and self-management to create a free wide platform using recycled modular structures adapting to a wide range of activities. The area will be transformed into a park using only the site's own resources and without the need for any expensive renaturalization measures. The programme includes the design of a temporary refugee camp in view of the potential worsening of the tidal flooding phenomenon (*acqua alta*) in the future caused by major climate changes. (G. Carli, R. Miotto)

pp. 54, 58: Giovanni Gabai, Quentin Georgelin, Jean-Loïc Nédélec, Ludovico Tiberio; **p. 55:** Marta Finotello, Cesira Roselli, Camino Sanchez Gonzales, Valentina Trevisanato; **p. 59:** Alice Covatta, Manoly Kaophone,

Niccolò Tosetto, Francesca Zalla; **p. 62:** Giuseppe Giordano, Elina Lecomte, Giulio Pellizzon; **p. 63:** Benoît Barnoud, Javier Puertas, Javier Serrano. *Lagoon Architectures*. Design Studio, Graduate Programme in Landscape Architecture, University Iuav of Venice, 2007–08, professors Renato Bocchi, Enrico Fontanari, Manuel Ruisánchez Capelastegui, tutors Alberto Bertagna, Sara Marini.

The workshop responded to the ideas competition launched by the Catalan magazine *2G* with a proposal for the contemporary city as "landscape" through the definition of the Venice Lagoon Park and its port on Sacca San Mattia. The project was developed around the concepts of "waste" and "project": once an epistemology of waste had been outlined, theoretical and interpretative instruments were applied to reappraise the construction of the Venetian lagoon system and put forward new scenarios focusing on the nature of this "archipelago of waste." The reflection upon this "unstable land" veered between the reinterpretation of the lagoon system starting with its islands and the definition of the said islands with respect to the design of the Venetian archipelago, applying head-on and reverse angle shots and "typological" and thematic scaling operations to macrostructures and microcosms.

pp. 66–99: Michele Lamanna, *Paesaggio negato*, 2009–11. © Michele Lamanna

pp. 106–14: Marco Scapin, *Accidental Waiting*; **pp. 115–23:** Sergio Bortolussi, *Food for Thought. Chernobyl, 25 Years After*. Graduation thesis, supervisors Alberto Bertagna, Enrico Fontanari, University Iuav of Venice, 2009–10.

The proposal for *Chernobyl*, a contaminated radioactive site extending over a vast area in three national states (Ukraine, Belarus and Russia) including a highly restricted physically enclosed core area (Reactor 4 of the Lenin Nuclear Plant), adopts different approaches or points of view. The aim of the project is to identify possible measures and strategies applicable on different scales and involving different actors. The priority is to emphasize the key role of the affected populations and the consequences of the disaster for future generations in the development of possible solutions and policies. The agricultural reuse of former farmlands in the exclusion zone; the creation of a protected "radioecology" reserve in the Polesia, Europe's largest wetland; the improvement of the touristic offer are all ways of revitalizing an abandoned and demonized area through the partition of a scenario. (S. Bortolussi, M. Scapin)